CLAMP SCHOOL
PARANORMAL INVESTIGATORS

Vol. 1

Written by
Tomiyuki Matsumoto

Illustrated by
CLAMP

HAMBURG // LONDON // LOS ANGELES // TOKYO

CLAMP School Paranormal Investigators Vol. 1
Written by Tomiyuki Matsumoto
Illustrated by CLAMP

Translation - Ray Yoshimoto
English Adaptation - Jamie S. Rich
Copy Editor - Amy Spitalnick
Design and Layout - James Lee
Cover Design - Gary Shum

Editor - Nicole Monastirsky
Digital Imaging Manager - Chris Buford
Pre-Press Manager - Antonio DePietro
Production Managers - Jennifer Miller and Mutsumi Miyazaki
Art Director - Matt Alford
Managing Editor - Jill Freshney
VP of Production - Ron Klamert
President and C.O.O. - John Parker
Publisher and C.E.O. - Stuart Levy

A  Novel

TOKYOPOP Inc.
5900 Wilshire Blvd. Suite 2000
Los Angeles, CA 90036

E-mail: info@TOKYOPOP.com
Come visit us online at www.TOKYOPOP.com

ISBN: 1-59532-091-1

First TOKYOPOP printing: September 2004
10 9 8 7 6 5 4 3 2 1
Printed in the USA

CONTENTS

CLAMP School Paranormal Investigators takes place in the famous CLAMP Universe, a self-contained, self-sufficient fantasy world of endless possibility. At the Universe's center is CLAMP School—a collegiate utopia—where the Paranormal Investigators reside. From kindergarten through university level, CLAMP School serves as a haven for overachievers and a paradise for prodigies.

The campus—nearly as magical as the students themselves—is shaped like a large pentagram, with a clock tower as its centerpiece. Surrounded by grassy parks and rivers, the campus also houses a subway system, hospital, bank, art museum, and much more! It's no wonder that the members of the Supernatural Phenomenon Research Association (Takayuki, Mifuyu, Yuki, Rion, and Koji) never want to leave.

Another important thing to know about *CLAMP School Paranormal Investigators* is that the manner in which characters address one another is essential to the overall personality and charm of the series.

Sometimes characters will call each other by their first name, sometimes they will use their last name, and sometimes they'll use either of the above with suffixes called honorifics. It might seem a little unusual at first, but you'll get used to it in no time. You see, in Japan, the way people address one another says a lot about their relationship. And, to make sure your reading experience is as authentic as possible, we've kept these naming conventions intact.

Below is a list of some of the honorifics you'll see in *CLAMP School Paranormal Investigators.*

-kun: Used as a familiar for someone of the same age or younger.

-chan: Feminine version of -kun.

-senpai: Used for upperclassmen and/or someone in an organization with more experience.

-san: Used among peers who are not intimate; the American equivalent is Mr. and Mrs.

Well . . . that concludes our lesson. I hope you enjoy *CLAMP School Paranormal Investigators,* one of the first books from TOKYOPOP's new and unique line of manga novels. Make sure to check out *Slayers: The Ruby Eye,* in bookstores now!

—nm

CLAMP SCHOOL
PARANORMAL INVESTIGATORS

Character Introductions

Takayuki Usagiya

High School Division, second year, Class B, age 16. The master of Koizumi-san. (She's a ghost and Takayuki's former maid.)

Mifuyu Mizukagami

High School Division, third year, Class Z, age 18. Get past her innocent face and airhead personality, and you'll find a master swordfighter who never goes anywhere without her ace blade, the *Kotetsu*, strapped to her back.

Yuki Ajiadou

High School Division, second year, Class A, age 16. Although a male in body, in heart s/he is a woman. Yuki, the Chairman of the Association, has teleportation powers and the hope of becoming a sensational actress.

Rion Ibuki

Middle School Division, second year, Class C, age 14. The daughter of a proper Shinto family, Rion was born in a shrine. The youngest in a long line of spiritual mediums, she is heir to a power that allows her to see spirits and read their thoughts.

Koji Takamura

Elementary School Division, sixth grade, Class A, age 11. A grade-school ninja born into one of Japan's most preeminent ninja clans, the Takamura family. Koji has an innate talent for the ninja arts; however, his physical stature has yet to catch up with his skills.

Prologue

BOOOOM!

The explosion rumbled through the tunnel, echoing off the concrete walls.

BOOOOOMMM.

The second one followed almost immediately. It was bigger, louder. It shook the students, making their brains feel like egg yolks in the shells of their fragile skulls.

"Watch out, *Senpai!*"

It was hard to tell who was shouting what in all the confusion.

Takayuki Usagiya felt a gust of wind over his head, the *whoosh* of a giant arm rushing by.

"Rion-chan! Get out of here! *Now!*"

BA-BOOOOOMMMM!

Rion Ibuki grabbed the side of her head, tightly clutching the two enormous pigtails that sprang from either direction. She screamed, "*Eeeeeeeeee!*"

BOOOOM.

One of the boys, a grade-schooler, broke from the group. He was wearing suspenders and shorts, the uniform of a child too young to be involved in something like this. He pulled several shiny objects out of his pocket as he rushed to Rion. "Hey, you beast!" he yelled. "Take this!"

SHUNK! SHUNK! SHUNK! SHUNK! SHUNK!

Five perfectly polished *shuriken*—deadly sharp ninja stars—sank into the monster's body. The sound they made was unpleasant, but then, so was the action itself.

"Forget it, Koji!" Takayuki said, rolling to the ground as another of the enemy's massive arms came slamming down at him. "Those won't work! What we have here is a Subway Train Monster!"

"Darn!" Koji shot a look at Takayuki, and the boy nodded back, affirming that the monster's attack had missed its mark. "What's it going to take to bring this thing *down?*"

Determining this was a problem best solved out of harm's way, Koji Takamura grabbed Rion by the arm and led her out of the tunnel.

As he looked back, Koji saw another one of the girls standing rigid amid the chaos. Her hair was pulled back into a braid, falling down her back, along the scabbard of the Japanese sword strapped there. He watched her reach back and draw the sword. Her movements were tentative, as if she wasn't quite sure of the viability of such a defense, yet showed the assured grace of someone familiar with her weapon.

"*Mizukagami-senpai!*" Takayuki was holding out his hand to her, the palm flat and facing out. "Don't do it! Even though the *Kotetsu* is a mighty blade, it's not enough to stop the monster!"

Mifuyu Mizukagami held her ground, but her eyes showed hesitation. "B-but . . ."

Takayuki's words were sinking in. She looked at the monster, and all the confidence drained from her face, replaced with the look of a child who has just dropped her favorite candy bar in the mud.

"Takayuki-sama!"

The voice came from behind them. A young woman wearing wide, round glasses and a vintage maid's uniform was flying down to them, seeming to manifest from the sky itself.

"You don't know what you're dealing with," the young woman said. "I sense a *ki* in that machine unlike anything I've ever experienced before. At least not like anything I've witnessed in something *living*."

"You mean it's not alive?" Takayuki asked.

"I'm afraid not."

The woman's revelation sent a fresh ripple of shock through the students. One in particular, a slender boy dressed in a girl's school uniform, had reached his breaking point. "I don't understand!" he screamed, his long, straight hair flailing wildly. "How did it go so wrong? Where did this monster come from? All we wanted to do was try out one simple spell."

Yuki Ajiadou's cries of protest went unnoticed, however, swallowed by the racket of the living Hell that had broken through the subway tunnel floor.

It had all started so simply.

"Now, then," it was announced, "our latest research project will be the Subway Vows."

They had gathered on the landing near the rooftop entrance to the CLAMP School High School Division Building. There were five students total, each representing a different year and a different class—and each with his or her own distinct interests. As individuals, they were just your average CLAMP School students, but as a group, they formed the infamous Supernatural Phenomena Research Association. Those who were in the know knew their names, and those who weren't may have heard them mentioned in whispers, but generally spent their lives safely sheltered from the sort of things the Association was formed to confront.

Yuki had made the announcement. He was acting as Chairman. "A big-time spell has come to our attention," he said, "and we're going to go to its source and verify its validity. To do so, we'll need to search the school's subway system. We'll also need to decide on the things we'll wish for."

Takayuki was on the outskirts of the group. He was cleaning his silver-rimmed glasses with the bottom of his shirt. "In other words," he said, putting the glasses back on, "we're going to have to stock up on subway tokens, because we'll need to ride every possible route. And if we repeat ourselves, then we'll have to start over from the beginning."

"That's right," Yuki confirmed.

CLAMP School Incorporated was Japan's largest private educational facility, with an unparalleled academic record. Located in the Tokyo Bay area, it sprawled across a plot of land measuring 3.2 kilometers in diameter and holding facilities unlike any found in other schools.

For instance, the campus grounds were covered by a subway system—a linear motorcar linking the varied sections of the school. It made a total of ten stops and could take any student wherever he or she needed to go.

As with any such community, CLAMP School had its own mythology. Urban legends arrived weekly, and they spread through the student body instantaneously. The latest popular belief was that if you visited each station in order, you would be granted one wish upon the completion of your journey.

"How can we even do that?" Mifuyu asked. If it had come from any of the others, it would have sounded like a pragmatic question, but Mifuyu's girlish looks, complete with pigtails, imbued it with a childlike quality not at all befitting the high school uniform she wore. "We're only supposed to ride the subway twice a day at the most. If we take *that* many trips, aren't we going to get in trouble?"

"She's right," added Rion, a middle-schooler sitting next to Mifuyu. "They scan our IDs every time we board. They keep track of when we get on and off. If the teachers notice, we're likely to get detention or something."

"Oh, well, I wouldn't worry about that," Koji laughed. Still in elementary school, Koji was the youngest of the Association. He was generally the last to speak up, yet was the most daring of the group. "There's a simple way around it, even if it is kind of cheating. All we have to do is gather all of our IDs, and every time one of us gets on the train, we hand security a different ID. They'll never check; you know how security is down there. I hear that's how the other kids who want a wish do it."

"Yes." Takayuki nodded, as if he knew this all along. "I say we reward you for your ingenuity, Koji. Everyone, hand over your student IDs. Koji is going to be our first passenger."

Everyone began fishing through his or her pockets and bags, pulling out IDs and passing them to Takayuki. Koji was stunned. He couldn't believe it was all happening so fast. "W-what?" he stammered. "Me? Y-you mean *me?*"

"You're the one who suggested the plan, so you should implement it. The person who comes up with the idea is the one who knows it best, right? I just hope you have a good wish. I'd hate to see the opportunity wasted," warned Takayuki.

Mifuyu placed a hand on Koji's shoulder. "Good luck, Koji-kun," she said with a reassuring smile. It signified her faith in him.

Koji just wished he had the same faith in *himself*. But, an assignment was an assignment, and he had no choice but to go through with it.

"All right then," he said. "If that's the way it's going to be, then my wish is . . ."

Now that he was in the very real danger of battling the Subway Monster, Koji couldn't believe he had come up with such a frivolous wish. Dodging the creature's deadly attacks put everything in perspective: "Aghh! With this monster in my way I'll never get my wish of the Hanshin Tigers winning the baseball championship!"

Half-sobbing, Koji hung close to his friends. Strength in numbers, and all that.

"*Back off!*"

Mifuyu swung her sword, the Kotetsu deflecting the steel bars the monster was flinging their way. Sparks crackled in the air as metal hit metal.

The Association boasted a strong showing of martial arts talent among its ranks. Mifuyu was a master swordsman, trained in the art of a warrior, carrying a blade with a heroic history. For his part, Koji was the latest in a combat lineage that extended centuries. He was the youngest member of the Sengoku ninja family.

Unfortunately, even if the monster understood this, it probably wouldn't have mattered much. The creature didn't seem to be easily intimidated, even though moments ago it had morphed from a subway train into the shape of a person. This mutated creature stood twelve meters tall, a towering achievement shadowing even Mifuyu and Koji's skills.

BOOOMMM!

The monster was moving in closer. Takayuki knew something had to be done if they were going to get out of there safely. They had to try every angle, no matter how seemingly impossible. "Rion-chan!" he shouted. "Look inside the Subway Monster! Do you see anything peculiar? Has something possessed it?"

"Not a possession, no," Rion replied. "It's not a spiritual *ki* . . . but I think . . . I think I sense the presence of a *fairy.*"

Rion withdrew into the shadows, searching for a spot outside the madness, somewhere quiet where her thoughts could be her own and could be controlled. As she closed her eyes, she tried to focus on the spirit of the creature, delving into the core of its consciousness. Rion was also from a prominent family, an honorable Shinto clan with a bloodline that produced some of Japan's most powerful spiritual mediums. She relished the opportunity to honor her ancestors by putting her family's gifts to proper use.

"A fairy?" Takayuki asked. "You mean like a soul spirit?"

"Yeah, probably. Or something like that . . . I think . . ." Rion wasn't yet comfortable with her powers, and she would hate to misinform her associates.

"Interesting," Takayuki said. "*Koizumi!*"

The ghost rushed to her master's side. "Yes, Takayuki-sama?"

Some might find it strange that Koizumi, who used be a living, breathing housekeeper in Takayuki's family home, continued to help him from the afterlife, adeptly performing her duties from beyond the grave. Yet, not the norm, this certainly was not the strangest thing in the Association's short history.

They say good help is hard to find, but the same could be said about good employers. Koizumi felt that once you find a good place, you stay—and so she did for many generations.

(Hey, who are we to judge?
The rationale worked for them.)

"Go to the Professor," Takayuki said, "and tell him what's happening. We need help and he's the only one who can give it to us. We've got to figure out how to stop this thing."

"Yes, sir."

Koizumi zoomed from the tunnel, flying at a speed impossible to track with the naked eye.

Standing in the thick of the chaos, metal bars swirling through the air, was Yuki, whose desperation was starting to get the best of him. He blamed himself for bringing his comrades into the tunnel and felt it was his responsibility to get them out of this mess. "I should have stuck with the UFO investigation instead . . . ," he sighed, "something that wasn't so risky. The trouble is, I didn't really want to. I was sure that this was the case we *had* to pursue."

The Invader from Space

It was a beautiful day.

It was one of those days where the weather was so nice, people—young ones, especially—couldn't resist seeking out a good time. There was no point staying indoors, there was so much to do. And since it was already July, there weren't any classes to go to anyway. The students at CLAMP School were free to seek whatever fun they desired! Even the students who regularly swam in the campus' indoor pool, the only place in Japan where it was summer 365 days a year, had an extra spring in their step. When it was swimming season, not even PE class was a chore, because you knew the hour would be well spent in the Emerald Ocean, a place that could give a "real" beach a run for its money.

"Are you ready, Senpai? Here we go! Serve!"

PLUNK.

"Back atcha, Rion-chan! Ha!"

SPLOOSH.

Rion and Mifuyu were tossing a rubber beach ball back and forth, setting up an impromptu volleyball game in the clear blue waves. Rion's yellow hair was tucked up under a swimming cap, while Mifuyu's dark braided locks let her capless hair dangle freely in the water.

The pool was so pleasant and the game so much fun, the pair could have stayed in the water all day. It felt like the most natural thing in the world.

"Rion-senpai! Mifuyu-senpai!"

The voice called to them from a distance. On the nearby shore, a small boy in blue swim trunks was waving at them. He had set out a white beach mat and was motioning toward various objects spread across it, including an open picnic basket.

"I've brought some *mitsuame* cream puffs!" he shouted. "They're made with the sweetest Mandarin bean paste you can get!"

"Okay, we'll be right there!"

"You're an absolute doll, Koji-kun!"

The girls ran out of the water, sprinting up the shore so quickly they didn't even mind getting slapped by the surge of hot air or pricked by the heat of the artificial sand. The giddy joy from the game had settled on their bodies like glitter, and they laughed as they scooped up the chilled silver bowls, digging hungrily into the fancy desserts.

Mifuyu looked up from her pastry, cream spread across her grinning lips. "It's too bad Takayuki-kun couldn't come with us," she said.

"Aw, you know him," Rion laughed. "It was his dorm's day for cleaning, and he wasn't going to skip out on that. That kid has some wacky priorities."

"I think it's great that Usagiya-senpai is so proper," Koji said. "I wish my neighbors were as considerate as he is."

Koji spooned a cherry from the cream puff and slid it into his mouth. He let the spoon dangle there, freeing his hands to scratch an itch on his defined cheeks. Those cheekbones were well-known among the co-ed population of CLAMP School. Many a girl had swooned thinking about them touching her own.

The roof of the Emerald Ocean had been fashioned out of glass so that students could enjoy natural lighting all year-round. It was also retractable, and on warm days it could be opened so the sunlight could tumble directly onto the simulated beach. Even though the high walls kept out the wind, there was always a breeze inside the pool area, causing the palm trees and hibiscus to gently sway. The breeze came off the artificial waves, their undulating rhythm producing the continuous illusion of summertime. All around the Association members, the sun sparkled, mingling its light with the sound of the other swimmers' elated voices. It was easy for them to lose themselves in this summer reverie, and altogether forget they were actually at school—and on a mission.

Koji leaned back on the grass, letting the sun splash across his face. As he stretched his arms over his head, he released a long, satisfied yawn. "It sure is peaceful here. Who says a student's life is rough?"

(Really, could you blame him for enjoying it?)

Ever since the CLAMP School Supernatural Phenomena Research Association had begun investigating otherworldly events taking place on campus grounds, none of the boys or girls in the club was able to get much downtime. Every time they completed one incredible case, another one, even more outrageous than the last, was waiting for them in the wings.

And so, with a little bit of rest and relaxation in their grasp at last, these three weren't going to waste any of it. Any thoughts of their paranormal caseload were quickly lost in the soothing sounds of the rippling water. This was, after all, what summer vacation was for.

"We've been burdened with such hard cases these days," Yuki-senpai had said, "with no time at all to just hang out together and have fun. So why don't we plan on going out and celebrating getting through another school year? I was thinking that a trip to the pool would be nice. It'd give me a chance to show off my new swimsuit."

Even if that last remark made it clear the suggestion wasn't entirely selfless, the other four couldn't deny their Chairman's idea was an attractive one.

Thus, it was all the more startling when they realized—
"Hey, where is Ajiadou-senpai, anyway?"

"Now that you mention it," Mifuyu mused, "Yuki-chan wasn't here when we arrived."

Rion sat up. She was only just noticing Yuki's absence, as well. "Come to think of it," she said, "I haven't seen him all day. Which is unusual."

All three of them felt bad for not being more aware. The fun-loving Yuki had come up with the idea of going swimming, so they really should have noted his absence much earlier. Particularly since they'd never known him to be so late. Yuki-chan was always the first to arrive at any party.

"You guys looking for someone?"

As if on cue, a familiar high-pitched voice pelted them from behind.

"Chairman!" they exclaimed. "Where have you been?"

"I was waiting for the dressing room to clear out," he said. "The kids in my class know me, so it's no big deal for them to see me in the girls' dressing room. On the other hand, students I *don't* know might feel differently."

"Oh. Yeah . . ."

Rion jumped to her feet and clapped her hands in excitement.

The Chairman had arrived—a vision of contoured loveliness. By all accounts, Yuki looked fantastic, beaming in his white, two-piece swimsuit. The upper half of the outfit was a sleeveless shirt dangling loosely over the chest, while the lower half was a fashionable version of the standard gym short variety. As if that weren't enough, a large, puffy (yet cute) brimless hat—the final touch of the original ensemble—cradled those gorgeous blond locks. It was a Yuki original, teen *haute couture* at its finest. Put simply, he looked like a dainty sailor in a halter top—simultaneously modern and retro.

"How adorable!" Rion squealed.

Mifuyu licked the cream from her lips (though, really, getting only about half of it). "You look incredible, Yuki-chan."

Yuki giggled, twirling around so they could see every angle. "Hee. Don'cha think?"

"Uh . . . well, I guess when you dress like that . . ." Koji paused. He knew he was about to put his foot in his mouth, but there was no backing out now. "That is, you look like a girl all right."

"Of course I look like a girl." Yuki snapped. "Is it my fault I had the rotten luck of getting stuck with some *boy's* DNA?!"

Yuki's face burned red with the heat of the insult.

"Never mind all that," he said, finally. "Isn't there a parfait or something for me around here? If you're going to treat the girls, good manners would be to buy some for *all* of them."

"Huh?" Now it was Koji's turn to blush. "B-but you weren't here, so I thought . . ."

"Don't make excuses! The proper thing to do is to go buy another. Don't worry. I'll wait."

"Y-yes, sir!"

Spurred on by Yuki's sharp reprimand, Koji took off like a shot, sprinting from the Emerald Ocean in the direction of the ice cream shop.

Mifuyu tossed Rion a look. They had both been struggling not to laugh, but as soon as their eyes met, there was no stopping it.

These four were all members of the Supernatural Phenomena Research Association, a secret society that operated out of CLAMP School.

Senpai Kyoko Karyuin, who had graduated the previous spring, was the original founder and ringleader of the Association. While she left to pursue a career at Nanigashi Bank, the new quintet of investigators was intent on maintaining her vision and solving the rash of supernatural incidents on campus. With the ascension of current Chairman Yuki, a candidate handpicked by Karyuin, the Association had gotten more aggressive with its endeavors. Namely, he was inspired to solve some high-profile mysteries so the Student Body Executive Committee would promote the group from Association to Club status. Yuki's deep-seated longing for the Association to win *official* acceptance was what drove him to chase one paranormal excursion after the next. Another one of the Chaiman's passions was acting. It was his lifelong dream to become a dancing, singing actress. He was even a proud card-carrying member of the Theater Society.

Yuki had been infatuated with images of glamour and womanhood since he was a young child. As a result, his Holy Grail was a profession that would let him perform as he saw himself—as a woman. Not only did the stage allow him to feel free, but it also made him feel normal. These feelings, combined with the heat from the spotlight and the energy from the audience, would constantly beckon him. It was this passion for performance that led to an event that would forever alter Yuki's life.

One day, while rehearsing for a play, he had worked himself into such an emotional frenzy that he fell off the stage. In the instant before hitting the ground, all he could think about was how much he didn't want to slam into the hard floor. The next thing he knew, he was across the room, standing on his feet. Somehow, Yuki had removed his body out of harm's way. It turned out that the kinetic energy released from the fall redirected and tripled in force, transporting his entire body to an altogether different location.

In other words, Yuki was able to swap himself and the space he occupied with another chunk of space of equal size, teleporting himself instantly from point A to point B.

There were many things in this world that science continually failed to explain, prodding some people to step outside its bounds to seek the answers. Having heard about Yuki's new development, Kyoko contacted him to join her Supernatural Phenomena Research Association.

After listening to what Kyoko had said about others experiencing things just as strange and inexplicable as he had, Yuki agreed without hesitation to become the new Chairman of the Association. From that day forward, he actively pursued a course of educating the world on the truth behind supernatural events.

Led by Yuki's charisma and leadership, the reinvigorated Supernatural Phenomena Research Association ushered in a new era of valiant action. Unfortunately, any official attempts to elevate the Association to Club status were shot down, and the general public remained ignorant of the Association's life's blood.

"Check it out. She's actually going to dive!" blared an anonymous high-pitched voice.

Yuki's taste buds tingled in anticipation of the imminent arrival of cream parfait. But a buzz of another kind was rising from the poolside crowd.

Koji came running through the gathering mass, thick trickles of sweat rolling off his face. "What's going on?" he asked.

He spun around, looking at all the students on the beach. One by one, they stopped what they were doing, stood, and looked to the far end of the pool.

"Is something happening?" he now asked.

Rion and Mifuyu had been reclining, enjoying the decadent satisfaction the desserts had left in their stomachs. But they, too, began to sense the hum of activity. Their ears perked up, hoping to overhear whatever was happening around there.

Koji finally saw it. "Look!" he exclaimed, pointing toward the far wall, in the direction of the diving boards.

The Emerald Ocean was a fully functional indoor pool facility, designed to handle a multitude of events. These ranged from your average school gym class to large-scale competitions such as diving meets. Several types of diving boards, all with varying heights, had been built at the deep end of the pool. The most impressive was the CLAMP School exclusive: a fifteen-meter platform, the only one of its kind in Japan. Most diving matches feature only five-, seven-, and ten-meter dives.

A fifteen-meter dive was part of a whole other athletic stratosphere, which is precisely why the board *never* got any use. Instead it pretty much collected dust and other random debris. Sure, it had seen its share of wet footprints, but usually they tracked to the platform's edge, turned around, and went right back down the ladder again. With all the fear and awe provoked by the board, it's no wonder that shortly after it was built, whispers began traveling through the school hallways. Kids talked in hushed tones. Teachers turned blind eyes. It was the biggest case of closeted mayhem ever! The rumor involved a legendary swimmer who had gone beyond simply approaching the great height of the diving board to dive so seamlessly off it, she appeared to be descending from the heavens themselves.

Urban myth suggested that this high dive wasn't really intended for use. One version of the rumor claimed that the board hadn't actually been built before the legendary swimmer's plunge; rather, it had been erected afterward, to honor her and commemorate this death-defying leap. Though no one who told this version ever explained what the diver had leapt off from, if not the fateful board. Still, no student had ever been seen climbing up there and exhibiting the kind of bravery required for such a plunge. Whenever anyone tried, there was always a rush of excitement, that maybe this time, it would happen.

As Koji and the others looked on, a thin girl stood at the edge of the diving board, staring straight ahead, her body poised as if she were going to jump. And no matter where you were inside the dome of the Emerald Ocean, her intense expression was clear to all.

"There's no way. That board is six stories high!" Koji declared. As a descendent of the Sengoku ninjas, he knew a thing or two about the limits of the human body. "Even if you're diving into water, the force of the impact could shatter your bones."

But then . . .

"Oh!"

"She's diving!"

The girl's feet left the safety of the platform, and she soared birdlike through the air. With her arms spread wide, and her grin even wider, her body pierced the sky.

The girl straightened herself. In one relaxed motion, her entire body formed a straight line, spearing the surface of the pool, then disappearing into the water, taking the surrounding air down with her.

The entire audience erupted into a huge cheer.

Even Koji, Mifuyu, and Rion found themselves applauding—

and they'd seen plenty of amazing things, being part of the Association and all. This . . . this was just inspiring.

"Incredible . . . !"

"It's just like Mishima-san, and that story where he was diving for fish."

Only one person seemed unmoved by the display—Yuki, who sat back, silently eating his parfait.

"Chairman . . . ?" Koji whispered.

One of the many students watching this death-defying event roused the Chairman from his reverie. "Something's not right," he said, then turned to the guy next to him. "How long has she been down there?"

"About a minute," the guy answered, glancing down at the waterproof watch on his wrist.

"That seems like a long time. Shouldn't she have surfaced by now?"

"Hmmm . . . now that you mention it . . ."

Another minute passed.

Then another. Three minutes.

"H-hey . . . should someone—?"

Four minutes.

Five.

Koji felt a surge of panic shoot up his spine. "Oh, no! Could she have drowned? Maybe she hit the bottom, and then—"

SHOOM.

A sudden gust of wind blew from behind him, followed by the sound of the sky itself being ripped.

WHOOSH.

And then there was Yuki, midair down from the platform, straight as an arrow, diving right into the water.

Koji's mind snapped to attention. "Of course! If she's drowning, someone has to save her."

Having sensed danger, Yuki leapt to his feet. Using the kinetic energy of his landing, he teleported himself to the point nearest to where the girl had last been seen.

However . . .

SPLASH.

"Phew!" Koji cried, taking a deep breath.

Just as Yuki entered the pool, the girl burst from beneath the surface.

Yuki bobbed up and down in the water. The girl didn't even notice him there. Instead, she casually swam to the side of the pool and climbed out. Grabbing a towel off a nearby bench, she dried herself with it, then wrapped it around her waist, ran her hands through her short straight hair, and shot off.

Yuki climbed out after her. As he got closer, he could see the porcelain white of her skin, brushed ever-so-slightly with faint hints of the sun. She wore a competition-style navy-blue swimsuit, which fantastically showcased her toned muscles, those of a real swimmer, and her sculpted features. Not only was she in top physical condition, but she had the athletic grace of a champion swimmer. Even out of the water, she moved fluidly, with the elegance of a ballet dancer.

Yuki was awestruck, to say the least. It was as if this girl had just stepped off the set of one of those old Hollywood movies he adored so much. The girl still took no notice of him, though, and with her chin lifted high, walked right past her new admirer.

But then . . .

As the girl brushed past, a single drop of water fell from her hair. It seemed to dangle in midair for a second, the light filtering through it, before gravity resumed and it sank.

"Ah . . ."

Yuki found himself instinctively following the trail of the drop with his eyes.

It tenderly hit the floor, quietly splashing, illuminated by the sun.

When Yuki looked back up again, the diver was already gone, having disappeared into the changing room.

Meanwhile, high in the skies above CLAMP School . . . a mysterious stranger had been silently watching the events at the Emerald Ocean. "I've found her. Finally, I've found her," escaped a barely audible whisper from the cryptic figure. "That girl has some set of lungs on her," he continued, pairing this final thought with a smug look, revealing some kind of private, personal victory.

The Supernatural Phenomena Research Association had gathered at their regular meeting place—the entrance to the rooftop of the high school, which was actually an abandoned section of the division, bare except for a small table and a few chairs made from metal piping.

Koji stood before his fellow members, dressed in his school uniform and doing his best to explain what had happened down at the pool. Takayuki, the fifth member of the Association, had not been able to go to the Emerald Ocean, and missed it all.

"I mean, I know the diving pool is deeper than your average swimming pool, but still . . . *five minutes!* That's a long time to be underwater. Everyone thought she was a goner!" Koji declared.

"Yeah, that's a pretty impressive amount of time to hold your breath," said Takayuki, impressed.

"She's new, a transfer student," Mifuyu said. It seemed like a less-than-essential detail when slotted next to the girl's achievement. "Of course, she's already joined the swim team, and they say she's a star candidate to lead the squad in the inter-high school tournament."

"Yeah, someone said her name is Sakimori Sumika-san," Rion added.

"And she's a third-year student in Class G," Koji said.

"You guys are pretty well-informed for only having *just* seen her," Takayuki remarked. He scratched his head, slightly puzzled. "You hadn't even heard of her before, and then you guys just *happened* to be there for her dive?"

The trio nodded.

"Come on, it's not like we *wouldn't* check her out after that!"

"How come?"

"Well . . . you see . . ." Rion seemed hesitant. "It's the Chairman . . . he's become . . . kind of a fan of Sumika-san."

"*What?!*" Takayuki couldn't believe his ears. "You investigated this girl because Yuki has a *crush?*"

The pool! The pool! The beautiful open-air pool!

Yuki bounded through the halls. He had changed back into his schoolgirl uniform and was clutching a bouquet of red, yellow, and white flowers. The Chairman was grinning from ear to ear.

In fact, he looked so incredibly giddy, it wouldn't have been a surprise if he instantaneously broke into a skip.

(And if you saw how happy he seemed, you'd understand
how infectious it was and would be grinning yourself.)

"Sumika?" one of the Class G girls had responded to his inquiries. "Oh, her . . . yeah, she's probably at swim practice or something."

"Oh?" Yuki asked. "Which pool would that be, then?"

"Probably the high school's open-air one."

Armed with this bit of information, so kindly bestowed upon him by an upperclassman, Yuki rushed toward where he could see Sumika once more.

The pool! The fantastic open-air pool! When she is done with practice, I will give her these flowers, and she will thank me, ask me to sit and talk, and then maybe we'll go somewhere to eat, but I'll be too happy to take even one bite!

Yuki couldn't recall a time when he felt so alive. Even the high school grounds, which he saw every day, seemed fresh and new now that he had met Sumika-san. As he picked the flowers, they almost appeared to be smiling back at him.

The summer sun paled in comparison to Sumika's skin, and though its rays were the warmest Yuki had ever known them to be, they could not equal the fire he felt inside.

What is this feeling? Everything seems so beautiful. The world is suddenly so strange, so fuzzy . . . could this be love?

Oh, my! How splendid! Something has been triggered inside my heart. Finally, I understand the way a girl loves!

Yuki looked up at the sky, past the sunshine, and saw what he could have sworn were all the stars in the universe. He trembled with passion. Yuki had always been a self-proclaimed lover of women, and all his friends had acknowledged him as such. Yuki had idolized women from a very early age, loving the very concept of womanhood more purely, more intensely, than anyone else ever had.

He was unclear when these feelings started to develop, since they seemed to have always been a part of him. As far back as he could remember, Yuki was *determined* to become a girl. He dressed like one, spoke like one, walked like one—single-handedly transforming himself into a version of all the great women he admired.

(While we're discussing this, let's give a nice round of applause for his kind and generous parents. They supported his wishes without complaint.)

The lovely actresses he saw in old movies inspired him to take to the stage as well, which was yet another reason behind him joining the Theater Society.

Unfortunately, no matter how hard he tried to *act* like a girl, he could never quite capture the full essence of femininity. He knew that in the end, it was up to his heart, a much more difficult aspect of the self to transform. Sadly, this rift between heart and body caused him traumatic self-loathing. He considered himself a failure and couldn't understand why he hadn't found a solution. Surely the women he admired were masters of their own souls—why wasn't he?

But now that Yuki had found the perfect girl, the living embodiment of his idealized image of woman, he became drunk with joy. At long last he had discovered what it felt like to love, the way a girl does.

For Yuki, Sumika was perfect. She was every dream realized.

From head to toe, she had the exact body he had placed on the pedestal of Perfect Womanhood.

Her dive had personified determination.

Finally, the noble air that surrounded her as she arose from the water—the guardedness, the poise—was that of a princess.

Every move Sumika had made held Yuki completely entranced. He'd heard of it, but couldn't believe he had found it: Love at first sight.

When Yuki arrived at the high school's open-air pool, the swim team practice was already underway.

He tried to sneak in through the entrance, but one of the team members saw him and stopped him. Yuki was about to panic.

"Are you here to watch? If so, you need to stay back. It's cool as long as you don't interrupt. And you should be careful not to get wet," the team member said.

Yuki breathed a sigh of relief. "Thank you. Uh, um . . . is Sakimori-senpai here?"

"Sakimori-san? Oh, yeah . . . I think she's resting somewhere, actually. She said she wasn't feeling well or something."

"Okay. Thank you."

The girl was about to say something else, but Yuki quickly darted away. *I'm in luck. This is my chance to get her alone.*

He frantically scanned the poolside for the object of his desire.

If she was going to rest someplace, she would probably go to the dressing room. Or maybe the showers?

Oh! Pardon me . . .

Yuki was opening each door, not even bothering to knock, peering in without shame.

Not here . . . nope, not here either. . . . Come on. Where could she have gone?

Charging into room after room and continually coming up with nothing was beginning to take his frustration and impatience to a new level. Nonetheless, he continued, moving quicker with each step, not really paying attention to where he was going. And before he knew it, Yuki found himself at the end of a rather dark corridor.

Where am I? . . . Uh-oh . . .

He was face-to-face with two hefty steel doors, both of which generated a low rumble and were potential hiding places.

Is this some kind of mechanics warehouse? Maybe there's stuff to clean the pool in here. . . .

CLAMP School had twenty-seven different pools, all of various sizes and shapes. Each pool was outfitted with the most up-to-date water treatment facilities. Everything was fully automated—one machine disinfected and cleaned the water, another removed any chemicals that could harm the students, and still another converted the hard water to soft water. These pools were so clean, they never had to change the water. They might even be an okay place to hide (if forced to do so).

But she couldn't possibly be in here.

Figuring it still couldn't hurt to look, Yuki gripped the door handle.

It's . . . unlocked, eh?

CREAK.

The door's hinges needed oil. They sounded totally creepy.

WHOOM. WHOOM. WHOOM.

Heavy sounds emanated from deep within the dark room. Yuki stepped inside with a bit of trepidation. Once his eyes adjusted, he noticed a large drainpipe running across the room. It looked almost like a chimney of a Tokyo bathhouse, lain on its side. And to top it all off, there were these large machines that clunked wildly and were covered with eerie flickering lights.

Sh-she can't be in here. Why would she—?

Feeling like he clearly did not belong, he began to hurry back out. Only . . .

Huh?

There was a strange metallic object in the far corner of the room. He couldn't put his finger on why it caught his attention, but it seemed totally out of place.

What's that?

He stepped closer. It looked like it had been built from a bunch of silver rings, intricately arranged and linked together. Inside the rings were three small, thin objects that resembled test tubes and stood upright.

While the flaming green lights of the machines had initially fueled Yuki's fear, they now stimulated his curiosity.

What kind of machine is that? It looks more like some sort of modern art sculpture.

Yuki couldn't resist. He had to touch it. There was no way he couldn't. Cautiously he stepped forward and reached out his hand. . . .

"Who's here?!"

Eek!

A voice came barreling from behind him. Yuki quickly pulled his hand back, as if he'd just touched something hot. He spun around, looking for the source of the voice.

And then there in front of him . . .

Yikes!

. . . flashing eyes!

No, wait. That was just a momentary lapse, a vision from Yuki's own imagination. Once his eyes readjusted, he took another look, realizing that the person who had cried out was a young girl, dressed in a swimsuit. Light from the hallway seeped in through the open door, transforming her into a delicate silhouette.

"Who are you?" she asked. "This room is off limits."

The girl took another step forward. Why wasn't she turning on the lights?

"Uh, w-well . . ." Yuki struggled for the words. "I got lost . . . hey!"

He felt that surge in his spine again.

"Sakimori-senpai!" he chirped, suddenly brightening.

"What?"

The girl looked surprised, obviously not expecting this invader to know who she was.

"I've been looking all over for you. I so terribly wanted to meet you. I'm your biggest fan."

"Huh?"

Sumika stood frozen as Yuki bounded toward her.

"I'd love to sit down and chat with you sometime. We can talk about your diving and the swim meets . . . that's what I wanted to ask you. Do you maybe have some time to hang out after you get done with practice today? I was thinking we could go for tea at the Café Terrace. What do you say? Please?!"

"Uh, well, I . . ."

Yuki placed the freshly picked flowers in Sumika's hand. She took a step back, and looked down at them as if she wasn't sure what they were or where they had come from.

"I'm sorry," she said. "I have something I have to do after school."

"Oh . . . I see."

Yuki's whole body sank. His shoulders dropped into a slump. There was no hiding his disappointment.

Sumika smiled. "I'm free tomorrow for lunch, though. I usually practice in the mornings and the afternoons, but if you don't mind, they give me a break in between. Is that okay?"

Yuki sprang up again, rocking on the balls of his feet. "S-sure! Thank you so much!"

He took Sumika's hands and clasped them firmly, the smell of the flowers wafting in the air between them.

SPLOOSH.

The sound of a tiny splash of water reverberated out of the darkness.

After that, there was nothing.

A lone figure was swimming silently in the diving pool.

It lapped the length of the pool completely underwater, rising by the wall near where it had dove in. It smiled, pleased with the effort. "Perfect," it said to itself. "Now I'll be able to dive anytime I want. . . . I didn't think I could make it happen, but now all doubt is gone."

The figure climbed out of the pool and disappeared into the changing room without saying another word.

"Chairman, I want to bring up an item of new business." Rion produced a report from her bag, and approached Yuki with it. "There was a UFO sighting on campus yesterday."

A sigh snuck out of Yuki's open mouth.

"Chairman?"

It wasn't like Yuki to be so lackluster, and Rion was used to inspiring more of a response than just a sigh. She studied Yuki's face for any kind of indication of what was going on.

Yuki rested his chin on his hands. With his elbows propped up on the desk, he gazed off into the distance.

It was after school, and the Association had gathered at the usual spot. Normally, their Chairman was a lot more animated for their meetings, full of pep and energy. It wasn't at all like him to be so quiet. It was actually quite strange.

"Uh . . . uh . . ." Rion wasn't sure what to say next. She was unable to release another word, or even another syllable.

Koji rescued her by cutting in. "Ibuki-senpai . . . it's no use trying to tell the Chairman *anything* right now."

"I guess. What's going on? Did something happen to Yuki-senpai? He seems so out of it."

"Oh, see, you missed it, because you arrived late, Ibuki-senpai. He's been this way all day long. It's like he left his mind back in his dorm room or something."

"Didn't you hear?" Mifuyu said, inserting herself in the conversation. "Yuki-chan went to talk to Sakimori-senpai during lunch."

"You mean the diver from the swim club . . . *that* Sakimori-san?"

"Yup."

Mifuyu gave Rion a wink. "Ohhhh." Rion finally understood. "Now that you mention it, he does seem oddly happy . . . even more so than usual."

"It was just the two of them," Mifuyu continued, "They dined at the Café Terrace and chatted the whole time. I didn't think it was possible, but he's an even bigger fan of hers *now* than he was before."

Takayuki rolled his eyes, but then quickly adjusted his glasses, as if trying to cover his response.

"Of course, there's got to be *something* we can do," Mifuyu said. "If he's going to keep this up, we're not going to accomplish anything today."

"Well, if you ask me, it's nice to have a quiet meeting for a change," Takayuki said, with a short, pained laugh. "We've been going from one investigation to another with hardly a break in between. Let's catch our breath while we can!"

"Well . . . I suppose . . . " Mifuyu looked to Koji to see what he thought.

Koji nodded at her. He understood her concern. "You're right," he said. "It's kind of creepy, actually. Ajiadou-senpai is usually so energetic. For him to be this quiet . . ."

"I *know!*"

CLANK!

The four of them froze. They looked like they'd just been caught doing something they knew they shouldn't have been doing.

Yuki suddenly stood up. Everyone else twitched, cowering, their eyes as round as beach balls. "I'm sorry. I can't stay. I have to go write my feelings in my diary before they float away," he said.

Koji was so shocked by the Chairman's declaration, he lost his balance and dropped to the floor. Yuki took no notice, though, and briskly walked out, not even pausing to look at his associates. But he didn't look worried or angry—on the contrary. A smile beamed from his face, the picture of pure happiness.

His slack-jawed colleagues were left both confused and worried as they soaked up the sound of Yuki daintily descending the stairs and humming an undecipherable tune.

XOXO

"Okay! Just a little more!" The CLAMP School Student Body Architectural Research Division members each motioned with both hands, directing the huge crane slowly entering the high school area.

"The plans call for it to be right about here."

A few of the student members, all of them wearing hard hats and so presumably part of the construction crew, were comparing the patch of land in front of them to the spot indicated on their blueprints.

The summer was just getting underway, and the Student Body Executive Committee was a long way from figuring out how to celebrate the end of a long, tough year of school. After an intense brainstorming session, they finally arrived at the verdict: They would build an outdoor dance floor and have their Annual Early Summer *Obon* Dance Party *outside*. It would be brilliant, a party to write home about . . . every centimeter of it decorated with traditional Japanese motifs.

And the kicker would be a computer-controlled light system they'd use to shift the party into high gear.

After all, the students deserved it, right? Their exams were over. Their classes were done. Yes indeed, another year down.

"*Bucho!*" one student called out, addressing his club president. "Is this where the crane should be?"

"It appears so," the Bucho responded. "Start setting out the building materials."

"Yes, sir."

Upon the director's signal, the crane operator went into action.

Sumika-senpai, sweet Sumika-senpai. I wonder if I'll make it in time to watch her practice?

Yuki had wandered onto the construction site, but his eyes were filled with dreams, not buildings. He was engaging in his new daily routine: watching Sumika practice at the Emerald Ocean.

"Hey, you!"

The crane began to lean to one side.

"Watch out!"

WHOOSH.

It was too late. The driver had not seen him, and the jaws of the crane opened, releasing a clutch of steel girders that plummeted straight toward poor, lovesick Yuki.

Sumika-senpai, sweet Sumika-senpai . . .

SLAM.

The girders crashed to the ground one by one, landing on the grass behind Yuki—one step behind each step he took, as if following him. He kept walking, lost in a daze, completely oblivious to the disaster that had nearly befallen him.

CRASH.

The last bar hit the earth behind him, spearing into the dirt and standing at an angle. Yuki hadn't once altered the rhythm of his step.

Sumika-senpai, sweet Sumika-senpai . . .

The entire high school construction crew stared on in wonder as the charmed boy walked out of sight.

"Bucho, is this where you'd like the statue to go?" a first-year art student yelled to his president from underneath the belly button of a giant Indian sculpture. He and some of the other students in the Art Club were carrying the statue's torso—its head and limbs would come later—looking for a place in the school garden to set it down. It was much bigger than they were, and to say they were struggling would be an understatement.

"Oh, yes, that's fine," the Art Club President said. "That's simply splendid. This should inspire some of the best sketches of the semester."

The Bucho was a short distance away. He used his hands as frames, holding them up in the air, getting the torso in the center of them, and viewing it from every angle.

Today was the biannual Art Club Outdoor Still Life Portrait Day, a contest for drawing sculptures placed in natural settings. Several torsos and other incomplete figures were placed in various spots throughout the high school gardens and forests. The statues were built to be ten times their normal size so that the young artists could be a good distance away from the subject and still compose their pictures properly.

"Now that that's done, let's call the club members and get started!"

Sumika-senpai, sweet Sumika-senpai. . . . Oh! I can't stand it anymore! Will I ever arrive at that cursed pool?

Yuki was minding his own business—continuing on his trek, passing the *bon odori* (summer festival) construction on the way through the gardens.

"What the—?"

At that exact moment, a wind blew in unexpectedly through the garden entrance, hitting a nearby replica of the *Venus de Milo* and pushing it off its base. As it fell, it bumped into the next statue in line, toppling it, and then that statue hit the next—the entire row of torsos and half-bodies took off tumbling, domino-style.

And, directly in the path of the falling statues, was Yuki. The statues kept tumbling and Yuki kept walking, totally oblivious.

It was as if everything was happening in slow motion. Some of the members of the Art Club stood frozen, shocked beyond movement, only able to let out a few meager screams and gasps, which fell on Yuki's deaf ears.

Darn it all. I can't wait. Desperate times call for desperate measures.

Yuki suddenly leapt into the air.

SLAM.

CRASH. *WHAM!*

An anonymous voice shot through the air: "Oh, no! That kid's been crushed! Qu-quick! We have to h-help him!"

The Art Club members ran to where Yuki had last been seen, completely panicked, mentally preparing themselves for total carnage, bloodshed—you name it.

But there was no sign of Yuki. In his place, only fragments of broken sculpture.

A shadowy figure had been watching Yuki's trail of danger, and it now snickered with regret. Making a quick retreat, it hurried off toward the Emerald Ocean.

SHOOM.

To be sure to make it to practice in time to see Sumika, Yuki had teleported himself across campus to a remote spot near the pool. Because he was so totally focused on seeing Sumika, he was still completely unaware of his near brush with death.

Okay, good. Nobody noticed me. Now, I have to find the swim team.

It was always good to take stock of your surroundings immediately after a teleport. Now that Yuki had his bearings, his mission would begin.

Or so he thought.

Yuki had landed at the maintenance entrance of the Emerald Ocean, and since no one's luck could hold out forever, it just so happened to be the day of the annual pool maintenance. Even though all of the pool's water was recycled, it had to be emptied once a year for various other reasons. Nonetheless, the tank used for this task was beyond immense: measuring twelve-meters wide, fifteen-meters long, and thirty-meters deep. And, as luck would have it, Yuki was straddling the corner of this beast-of-a-tank.

SLIP.

Yuki could no longer feel the floor beneath him. The sensation came over him suddenly, knocking him off balance.

Huh? What's happening? What's going on?

He felt as if he were flying.

Or more accurately, as if he had been lifted up, only to be dropped in the same instant. And he was falling faster than he'd ever fallen, faster even than the freefall ride at the amusement park.

Whaaaa—? Eeeeeeeeeeeee!

Unable to comprehend what was happening to him, events turning far too quickly for him to grasp, Yuki began to panic, completely forgetting he could get himself out of this mess the same way he got in—teleportation.

Before he could scream again, however, a beam of light burst into the tank from the main entrance. It encapsulated Yuki's body and halted his descent.

Finding himself floating ten centimeters or so above the very bottom of the tank, Yuki passed out.

At that same moment, the other four members of the Supernatural Phenomena Research Association were still trying to carry on with their meeting. They sat around the meeting room in their metal pipe chairs, not saying a word, barely moving, whiling away the time.

CRUNCH.

Takayuki placed some snacks on the white tablecloth that Rion had spread over the table. Takayuki was in charge of bringing munchies, a job he took very seriously. Mifuyu was a bit hesitant at first, but eventually she reached out for a bag of *senbei,* grabbing one of the Japanese crackers and taking a small bite.

Koji was no longer able to stand the silence. "When you think about it," he mumbled, instantly grateful to himself for making some noise, "these meetings don't have quite the same pizzazz without the Chairman."

"Too true," Takayuki agreed, folding his arms to show he meant it.

"It's like," Koji continued, "not having him here, makes me see more clearly how he really is the one that leads this Association."

"This is more like the old days, to be honest, back when Karyuin-senpai was still here," Rion whispered, a bit of nostalgia lacing her voice. "In those days, all of our investigations were on paper. It was just research, speculation, and report filing. Report after boring report on the most exciting supernatural things."

From the very beginning, the members of the Supernatural Phenomena Research Association were bound completely by their interest in the supernatural. They didn't join any other clubs, and spent most of their days doing typical student activities. At first, their work was simply an extension of their homeroom duties and brought with it very little in the way of satisfaction or achievement. Before Yuki, it was scarcely more than an excuse for drinking tea and telling ghost stories.

"This blows," Mifuyu blurted out, her mouth full of senbei.

"Yeah," Rion said. "When Yuki-chan became Chairman, it was tough keeping up with him, but at least we started having fun."

Everyone nodded in agreement.

"He can be crazy and out of control," Rion continued, "but it's just a sign of how exciting the Association can be."

"And more than anything, his goal is always clear," Koji said brightly. "He has the best intentions for us and never forgets his goal—that we will one day become a full-fledged Club."

"And we aren't researching stuff for no reason," Takayuki added. "He deserves a medal just for getting our lazy butts to work together."

"Even if sometimes he does wear those butts out!"

Everyone laughed at Rion's comment, but after the giggling resided, she added, barely audible, "I do hope he comes back soon."

Everyone nodded in unison again.

The room returned to silence.

But then, at that very moment . . .

"What are you all sitting around for? C'mon! Let's get this meeting started!"

Yuki's voice came bubbling up from the bottom of the stairs.

"Chairman?"

"Yuki-chan?"

"Come on, you slackers! If you're going to sit around and stare into space, then at least look for something. Tell me about this UFO incident."

"Uh, yes, sir."

All four of them were taken aback as Yuki bounded energetically up the stairs, but as the meeting room filled with his familiar enthusiasm, they all just as quickly breathed a sigh of relief. Their Chairman was back.

"So, let me see if I got this right: The UFO flew in a zigzag pattern, heading toward the east end of CLAMP School. . . ."

"That's correct, Chairman. I checked with the Astronomy Department, and according to their surveillance of the incident, the object disappeared at the campus' 1.8-kilometer mark."

Rion was reading the report she had prepared several days before. It was a preliminary research project that Yuki had commissioned from her before he became obsessed with his Sumika worship rituals.

"There haven't been any reports of missing aircraft in the area," Koji noted.

"At present, it's hard to believe that it was something as ordinary as an airplane," Takayuki scoffed.

"Its flight pattern was unnatural," Yuki said, "so you're right, we can't assume its disappearance would follow any normal logic either."

Yuki pondered this statement for a moment. Then his eyes lit up, as if something had just dawned on him. "What we need are some witnesses!" he exclaimed. "Koji! Go and find who was on that side of the campus at the time of the sighting and get them to tell you everything they remember about the UFO's shape and flight patterns. The more details, the better."

"Yes, sir."

"Rion-chan, Mifuyu-chan, continue grilling the Astronomy Department. Pick their brains for as much scientific data on UFOs as you can. We need hard facts, real information, so that we can determine whether *this* UFO is for real, or if it's some kind of man-made object, or something else altogether."

"Yes, sir."

"Leave it to us."

"Takayuki-chan, I need you to do a computer analysis on all the data that our team brings in. Cross-reference it with everything until you've got the identity and origin of this thing. I'm sure the current info isn't sufficient, but you should at least be able to deduce a starting point based on data from past UFO sightings."

"Okay!"

"He's amazing," Rion whispered to Mifuyu.

"Yeah, he's even more bossy than usual," Mifuyu whispered back. "He just sprang right back into action. I wonder what happened."

Just when they thought Yuki's leadership had drifted away, it had snapped back stronger than ever. They were normally impressed by his vision, but were even more blown away now.

The more he thought about it, though, something didn't sit right with Koji. "The thing is, Chairman . . ." He hesitated. "Well, what are *you* going to do, exactly?"

"Me? Uh . . ." Yuki pondered what he was going to say. "I'm going to the high school open-air pool."

The group was shocked. What was Yuki saying?

"I found something there," he explained. "Maybe the UFO left it, I don't know. Anyway, let's get cracking. We'll regroup back here tomorrow morning before classes and compare notes."

Before the last word was even out of his mouth, Yuki was gone, disappearing down the stairwell in a flash.

The rest of the Association wasn't really sure about what had just transpired. They just stood there and looked at one another, hoping an explanation might spontaneously erupt from one of them.

❧ ❧

Whoaaaaa . . . w-what am I doing?

Yuki stopped. He looked around to see if anyone had seen him. He was sneaking back to the machine room, where he had last run into Sumika. Yet, despite his body understanding where he was going, his brain wasn't quite with it. Yuki's thoughts were on something else entirely.

Ever since I fell into the Emerald Ocean's storage tank, I've had an irresistible urge to investigate the UFO . . . and now I'm sneaking back into the machine room, even though I know it's off limits. . . . What's going on with me?

As doubts raced through Yuki's mind, he still continued moving closer to the machine room. Had he lost control of his own body? Had something else, someone else taken over? Not being in touch with his feelings or actions was foreign to Yuki. He always let his conscience be his guide.

Yuki lived his life according to his gut, which meant he didn't always take the most logical courses of action. But it also meant he generally had some idea of what he was doing. Even though this wasn't the first time he had acted on something his brain told him not to, it seemed different now. In the past, he had been bold, rash even, but he always remained focused on his goal. Now, however, the things he was doing, the stuff he had said to the Association—these were altogether out of his league.

In his heart, he could feel that something wasn't right. A lot of what was happening wasn't supposed to be happening. Sure, the fall into the empty tank was a result of his own carelessness, but ever since it occurred, he felt almost like he had become someone else.

While reason indicated he was acting under his own power, his emotions spied inconsistencies. It was almost as if he were no longer the girl he saw in the mirror every morning, but instead a second Yuki had somehow been born inside him.

You know, I don't remember getting out of there. How did I escape the tank?

Yuki hit rewind on his memories, searching back for the moments he was missing.

When I fell, everything went black, and I couldn't think straight . . . but when I came to, I was on the bottom of the tank. I thought I had maybe teleported without knowing it, and that I had slowed down the energy of my fall.

His footsteps echoed in the corridor. He shook his head, trying to shake something loose.

No, that's not it. I can't teleport unless I specifically have a place in mind where I want to go. I had never seen the tank before, and the way I was freaking out while I was falling, it just doesn't add up. There's no way I could have made such a precise jump.

Yuki cast back further, thought harder. There had to be an answer.

Wait a second . . . there was a voice. . . .

It was the very last thing he remembered before he had blacked out.

I felt as if I was being enveloped in something warm and soft . . . a hovering sensation, the exact opposite of tumbling through the sky.

And then—*huh?*

Yuki stopped short. He was now standing in front of the same machine room, his feet seeming to have brought him there instinctively.

This is it. This is the place I was intending to investigate.

Yuki steeled himself.

CLICK, CLICK.

The door was locked.

He gripped the doorknob tightly and braced himself by placing his foot against the wall. He gave another shove, putting his shoulder into it. The door popped open, and Yuki was back in the machine room.

It was in this corner. . . . That's where I found the mysterious object.

He looked at the machines. One in particular looked familiar, and he went to it.

Is that . . . ?

The machine was still humming, emitting the same low sound.

The mysterious object, however, was nowhere to be found.

Strange. I could have sworn it was right here.

He scanned the room a second time. Then a third.

This is definitely the room . . . so where did it go?

SOMEONE MUST HAVE TAKEN IT.

You're right. Someone must have taken it.

IT WAS TAKEN BY SOMEONE WHO KNOWS YOU'VE SEEN IT.

Yes. They needed to hide it quickly once they knew I'd seen it.

The explanation seemed plausible, and Yuki was satisfied with it. Only the way it had come to him still troubled him.

Hold on a second. Did someone say something just now?

He scanned the room a fourth time.

Yuki was still alone.

That was strange, wasn't it? Oh, well . . .

Yuki reached his arms to the ceiling and stretched.

It doesn't matter. It all makes enough sense as it is. I've got other things to do.

WHOOSH.

Yuki jumped back.

W-what was that?!

Yuki was surprised to find his leg muscles tensing up. His whole body was changing its posture, as if preparing to retreat. He took a step back.

What the—?

A shaft of white light pierced the room, landing exactly where Yuki had just been standing. The concrete floor there began to singe, and the air filled with an acrid, burning smell. Smoke began to billow up from where the light hit. The concrete was definitely beginning to smolder.

"Who's there?!" Yuki cried out.

He spun around. All that remained was the sound of footsteps, as if someone had been running away from the door.

But no one was there. Not even the smallest hint of a person.

Is someone out to get me?

Yuki quickly hurried out of there. He decided for now it was best to leave the open-air pool and return to the center of campus. He didn't like being chased off, and his face showed it.

Someone attacked me, and with a laser, no less. Who would go to such trouble? What for?

Yuki was walking beneath the still, green poplars. There, in the quiet all around him, his need for an answer became even more desperate.

How did I sense that I was being ambushed? Was it because of my experiences with the supernatural? It can't be. I don't know how that would have given me the superpowers to dodge a laser.

The more he thought about it, the less sense it made.

Who would even be able to use a weapon like that at CLAMP School? I've never heard of such a thing. Have they no shame, doing something so totally inappropriate in this kind of environment?

Yuki's anger was starting to boil over.

Someone had *shot* at him—without any obvious reason. At least shooting with some kind of rationale makes sense. But this . . .

I have to stay focused here. This is no time to lose my cool.

He took a deep breath. Yuki needed to rethink what had just happened, this time from a different angle. Sometimes a new vantage point could make all the difference in the world.

Take it easy. Stay calm. The fact that I was shot at means that I did something to put the shooter at a disadvantage. So, what could that be?

Sitting down on a nearby bench, he folded his arms, bit his lip, and furrowed his brow in deep concentration.

Could it be that someone was mad I had snuck into the pool? Or maybe . . .

"Chairman!"

ULP!

Yuki leapt from the bench, feeling like his heart was a couple of centimeters behind, back where it was when he was sitting.

"Don't be scared, Chairman. It's just me, Koji."

Koji poked his head out from behind the bushes.

"K-koji? What are you doing back there?"

Koji looked at him like he had lost his mind. "Come on, Chairman. You're the one who told me to gather intelligence about the UFO."

"I didn't tell you to do it in the shrubbery! Have you been skulking around the high school division all this time?"

"Yes, sir."

Yuki sighed. "Yes, of course you would be. I'm sorry."

"It's okay," Koji laughed. "I just wanted to tell you something quite interesting that a passerby told me."

Koji noted the quizzical look on the Chairman's face and was perplexed by it. As Koji spoke, he pondered Yuki's strange expression, stumbling on some of the words as a result.

"This student was a member of the Environmental Science Appreciation Club, and it just so happens that on the day of the UFO sighting, this person was flying a research balloon to collect environmental data. The air samples the balloon collected yielded an inordinate amount of deuterium, a form of heavy hydrogen."

"Deuterium? You don't mean the stuff they use in nuclear fusion?"

"That's exactly what I mean . . . even if I don't really understand it. But that's what this kid said it was."

Heavy hydrogen, commonly known as deuterium, is a substance that is two-to-three times denser than regular hydrogen molecules, and it's used as an ingredient in nuclear power. Known as "the fourth fire," nuclear fusion is the process used to make a hydrogen bomb (and it's also a highly efficient fuel source). The sun itself is a giant nuclear fusion reactor.

Yuki knew that deuterium didn't show up just anywhere, unlike say, solar power. It can occur naturally, but only under certain conditions. Even in an atmosphere containing tons of hydrogen, it occurs only at a rate of about 0.015 percent.

"Don't you see?" Koji insisted. "This explains everything. If the UFO emitted this deuterium, then it *proves* that whatever the object was, someone must've *made* it. It's an amazing breakthrough in our case!"

Yuki wished he could feel as excited as Koji. But he couldn't help wondering, if this UFO were indeed a vessel powered by nuclear fusion, why would it release so much of that fuel into the air? Was it simply exhaust?

Then something occurred to him.

So . . . deuterium is made from hydrogen. And water is a product of hydrogen and oxygen. So, according to the Transitive Property of Equality, deuterium can be produced from water, right?

Koji could actually see the Chairman's brain working. As each thought lead to the next, Yuki grew more and more engaged. His glazed, upward-turned eyes and softened jaw were a giveaway that something big was taking place in that head of his.

"Sir? What's going on? What are you thinking?"

The words went right past Yuki. His mind was too busy to hear them.

The mysterious object I found was stuck to the pool's cleaning machine . . . so what if the object was a device used to convert water into deuterium?

The shock of Yuki's discovery registered on his face.

That's it! It all seems so clear now that I have the pieces. Except . . . b-but—

"Chairman . . . ?"

The eyes twinkling in the dark.

The unusually long time submerged underwater.

The lone witness . . .

"Koji!"

"Gah!" The outburst jolted Koji back half a step. "W-what is it?"

"You're on the right track, Koji. I need you to stick with it."

"Huh? Uh, okay."

Koji wasn't used to such spontaneous praise from the Chairman.

"You've inspired me. I need to check something out. I'll fill you in on everything tomorrow. Good luck!"

Yuki dashed off, took a bit of a skip in the air—

POOF!

Koji watched Yuki teleport out of sight. He truly had no idea what had just happened or what he had inspired.

All he could do was wave limply at the spot that just a second ago had held his friend.

Darkness.

Silence.

The fifteen-foot dive platform at the Emerald Ocean.

Dressed in a bathing suit, Yuki took several deep breaths in a row in an attempt to calm his beating heart.

If I'm right about this . . .

Yuki did one last, careful check of his waterproof flashlight before stepping out onto the platform.

Closing his eyes and straightening his stance, he concentrated on the water.

And then . . . he jumped.

While he barreled downward, the G-Force over-powered the energy gathered during the fall, and in a blink, he had transformed the G-Force into teleportation energy. A section of water at the bottom of the pool, the exact volume of Yuki's body, instantly switched places with him.

Whoa.

The sudden convergence of water pressure nearly caused Yuki to pass out.

Steady.

He shook his head, trying to regain his composure. Yuki switched his flashlight on.

That's it. . . .

His eyes followed the shaft of light down to the pool's drainpipe. Just beyond the sturdy metal lid, he saw a familiar silver glow.

It was the shape of several interlocking rings connected in a beautiful formation.

I knew it.

THAT'S IT. THIS IS THE DEUTERIUM CONVERSION DEVICE.

That voice . . .

Yuki couldn't believe his ears. "Who's there? Who is it? How are you talking to me?"

I'M RIGHT HERE.

That didn't help. Yuki had no idea where the voice was coming from and who it was talking to. This far underwater, it should've been impossible to hear anything, yet he was clearly aware someone was speaking to him.

And then . . . the realization . . . it struck him like a kick in the eye.

"Are you talking to me from . . . inside me?"

AHHHH, NOW HE GETS IT.

It made sense now, the way his thoughts and the voice echoed one another.

THAT'S RIGHT. I'M BROADCASTING FROM INSIDE YOUR OWN BRAIN.

Just as the voice said that, Yuki remembered everything.

It was all finally adding up: the fall inside the tank, the laser light that shot at him, the thing that had enveloped his body.

And the voice . . . that was the first time Yuki had heard it. "Are you all right? I used a part of your powers to stop your fall. It took everything I could muster to prevent you from smashing into the plaster. I'm sorry to take such drastic measures, but it was necessary."

"What? How so? You saved me?"

"In a manner of speaking, yes."

"I would thank you, but I don't know who you are—or why you would do such a thing."

"I need to ask you a favor."

"A favor?"

"That's right. I need you to allow me to stay inside your head for a little while. A temporary residence."

"Say what?"

"I won't bother you. I won't require any of your body's energy. I just need a place to stay, just for a bit."

"W-w-why?"

"I need to investigate."

"In-investigate?"

"That's correct. I need to locate an alien life form that has invaded your world—the Third Planet—and inserted itself into your society in this area. I wish to locate this alien so that I may expel it."

"An alien? Like from outer space?"

"Precisely."

"W-would this have anything to do with the UFO spotted flying over campus a few days ago?"

"You are a smart one. I have chosen well. I issued warning signals to the invader's vessel when it entered the Third Planet's atmosphere, and when it did not respond, I had no choice but to force it down."

"No way!"

"This invader has infiltrated your system in order to repair its vessel, this thing you call a *UFO.* I must not allow it to succeed."

"I get it. Time is of the essence. But why do you need me? Can't you just nab this thing yourself?"

"Unfortunately, no. Galactic Law says we are not allowed to make direct contact with your people. As a result, we are forced to use less-conspicuous methods."

"So when this is finished, you'll put me back to normal?"

"Just as I found you. You won't remember a thing."

"Well, shoot . . . and this was going to be my big chance to meet an extraterrestrial."

"I wish I could satisfy your desires, but your civilization is still extremely primitive, and there is a risk of self-annihilation if we overstimulate your species."

"All right, all right, I understand. If that's the case, who am I to argue?"

"So, you will help us?"

"Of course, only there's one condition."

"What's that?"

"You show me your true identity."

"But your memory will be erased. What would be the point?"

"I'd still know, if even for a second. I have to satiate my intellectual curiosity. Besides, when you ask *this personal* of a favor, you have to at least tell the young lady helping you out your name. It's common courtesy on my planet.

"Come on. How about it?"

"All right. I accept your condition. I am . . ."

XOXO

"So, do you remember now?" the voice asked.

"Completely. This machine belongs to the alien invader you were searching for?"

"That's correct. The creature used the machine to make deuterium out of the pool water from the Emerald Ocean. It was converting the water into fuel to power its vessel."

"So, in other words, it was ripping us off."

"In a manner of speaking . . . yes."

"Well then, are you going to destroy this machine?"

"As soon as the interloper is apprehended, we will eliminate its device. But not until then."

"Oh, by the way, you wouldn't mind me grabbing a breath, would you?"

Yuki scrambled to the surface. He had reached his lung-capacity limit.

"Phew!" He sucked in a fresh mouthful of air that, from the look on his face, seemed as if it could have been candy.

"Watch out." The voice left Yuki with one final admonition before it disappeared.

VOOM.

Instinctively, Yuki lunged to the side. A white shaft of light seared through the water in the very spot he had just emerged from. Another instant and he would've been toast.

SIZZLE.

Behind him, a large volume of water boiled and evaporated.

"Consider yourself lucky," a girl's voice hissed from the poolside. "I won't miss again."

"Sakimori-senpai!" Yuki cried out. "Or, to be more precise, whoever is borrowing Sakimori-senpai's body right now."

Illuminated by the moonlit glow seeping through the slats of the retractable roof was Sumika. She was holding a small object resembling a pistol and was dressed in her familiar blue swimsuit, which Yuki assumed she wore because of her underwater "work" with the machine.

"So, it was you all along." Yuki had suspected this from the start, but it felt terrible to finally say it aloud. "When I stumbled on your fuel reactor in the machine room, you were the only person who saw me."

"Interesting," she said. "I wouldn't have expected you to figure it out. You're an even bigger danger than I originally thought. It sure is a pity to kill such a smart boy like yourself."

Sumika—or rather, the alien who had taken over her body—slowly raised her pistol and pointed it at Yuki.

"Stop! I insist that you do your dirty work with someone else's body. I can't bear being harmed by my sweet Sumika."

"And that's what will make this kill even sweeter. Destroying someone who you know adores you is a perverse thrill, but one I definitely look forward to."

SHOOM.

The white light pierced Yuki's chest.

"Now with that troublemaker out of my way, all I'll have to do is retrieve my machine and load it back onto the ship." A golden light flashed above Sumika's head. This sudden, unforeseen illumination—could it be a snafu in her master plan?

"Battle armor *on*," rung Yuki's full-bodied voice from across the swimming area, as if he hadn't just been zapped by a mondo beam of light.

The glow was so bright, Sumika had to avert her eyes. "Oh, no!" she screamed. "I didn't think you'd be able to teleport in time. Your body can't still be conscious?"

What Sumika didn't realize was that the Yuki who appeared before her wasn't the same Yuki who had worn his fabulous bathing suit mere moments earlier.

Yuki was now all armored up, bound in brass from head to toe. The protective plates that covered his right arm, the left side of his head, and his left breastbone, shone as bright as a polished penny. It was obvious that Yuki, though looking more rugged than usual, felt just as comfortable in this ensemble as he would in an evening gown. He owned this look just like he owned all his others.

(That's one versatile fellow.)

"Wh-who are you?"

The fake Sumika shifted her voice back up to match the real Sumika's.

"I am Outer Space Milky Way Police Force Officer No. 192!" Yuki declared.

"What?!"

Sumika took a couple of steps back. She was completely shocked by this turn of events.

"Th-then you're the one who attacked my ship?"

"That's right." Yuki said. "I'm the one who cut your little invasion off before it could even begin."

"W-why you—!"

SHOOOM.

Sumika extended her left arm and lifted her palm up toward Yuki, violently discharging a beam of white light from her now-tainted hands.

CLANG.

The armor on Yuki's arm blocked the attack, the laser's energy dispersing harmlessly into the air.

"It's useless," Yuki said. "Your weapons cannot defeat me."

"No, that can't be!"

VWOOM.

This time, the light emerged from Sumika's right arm, extending into a sharp blade humming with electricity.

"If a blunt attack doesn't work, then we'll just go with something a little more precise. Your body already fell for mine, and now it's going to fall . . . to pieces."

"How presumptuous of you."

Yuki's body was taking to the role of Space Police Officer quite naturally, almost as if he had been one in another life.

(Hey, ya never know.)

A smirk slithered across his lips as he placed both fists on his hips and cockily raised his chest.

"By Milky Way Space Law Article 1, Number 28," he announced, "you are forbidden from making contact with unapproved species of any primitive planet's civilization."

"Shove it!" Sumika leapt high into the air, pointing her blade down, aiming it straight at Yuki's neck. The intent was deadly, but the execution a failure, as Yuki teleported to avoid the strike.

"Eraser Blade!" Yuki had barely gotten the words out before a blade of red light rose out of his palm.

"Grrrrr!"

"Eraser Z Beam!"

Working by command of Yuki's voice, the crimson weapon went into action, shearing through the fake Sumika's body—seeming to slice it in half.

"Ugh . . ."

The body of Yuki's beloved stumbled, fell to its knees, and slowly started to tip toward the pool.

Yuki heard that familiar voice from inside himself.

"Don't worry, friend. The girl is unharmed. I merely extracted the parasite life form from her body and exiled it back to its own dimension. The host will regain consciousness in time."

❧ ❧

The next morning, the Association gathered at their usual meeting place, just as they had agreed. You could cut the air with a knife, so thick was the tension in the room. Each member of the group eyed one another, all worried about disappointing their colleagues.

"And so, we weren't able to find any useful information related to the UFO reports," Mifuyu said.

"It's no good," Takayuki mumbled. "Dead end after dead end."

"Mifuyu-chan and I talked to everyone in the Astronomy Department, and there just weren't any new leads," Rion said. "I think Takayuki is right. This is going nowhere, and in the meantime there are other assignments waiting."

"Yeah, it might be a good idea to move on," Koji agreed. "We could always start digging into the story about the Subway Wish Fulfillment Rituals."

"The Subway Wish Fulfillment Rituals . . . ?" Mifuyu was obviously in the dark on this one.

Koji jumped from his seat. "Yeah, if you ride the full length of the school's linear motorcar service," he said, "while carrying a piece of paper with your fondest wish written on it, they say that your wish will come true."

"What we need is a plan," Takayuki said.

Rion, Mifuyu, and Koji immediately began studying all sorts of available and not-so-available campus maps—every one they could get their hands on. The prospect of something new was invigorating.

Yuki, on the other hand, was lost in his own sea of thoughts.

I wonder what it is . . . something's still bugging me. I feel like I had something I really needed to accomplish, but then yesterday it went away . . . but what could it have been?

An article in the student newspaper with the headline:

Seventeen-Year-Old High School Student Becomes New Swim Team Star

was dropped haphazardly on the desk in front of Yuki, who remained pretty much unfazed by the news.

Outside the window, the summer sky stretched across the horizon like a cat waking from a long nap. If you looked really hard, you could see the beginning of a wee light flickering in the corner of the sky. But hesitate just one moment and the light might disappear just as unexpectedly as it had arrived.

Intermission

The man of ultimate insight, otherwise known as the Professor, drummed his pen on his head as he tried to make sense of everything.

"Let me see if I'm getting this right. You're saying the subway train houses a spirit, and that spirit somehow found out kids were using it to get their wishes granted, so it decided to get in on the scam and fulfill its wish of becoming human?"

"Say *wha*—?" Koji blurted out. But when he tried to follow that up, he felt like something had wrapped its hand around his tongue, and the words wouldn't form.

"So," Mifuyu said, trying to fill the silence, "you're telling us that because we interrupted the train's ritual before it could get to the end of its wish, it only partially came to life? And now it's a living machine?"

"Well, if we are to believe my theory, then yes, that's exactly what I'm telling you," intoned the Professor.

"You've gotta be kidding," Yuki exclaimed. "We didn't interrupt it on purpose. We just happened to be investigating the whole wish-mumbo-jumbo thing when it passed by."

"Maybe so," the Professor said, clasping his hands behind his head. "But who's the one responsible for causing the car to jump the tracks because a certain someone was complaining that it was taking too long to move?"

Koji shot Yuki a begrudging look.

"Well, it did get us a couple of answers," Mifuyu said, easing the tension. "Now we know that the reason the school computers and electrical equipment were going haywire was because of that lightning bolt that struck the campus."

"Th-that's right!" Yuki shouted, sweat splashing off his forehead. "That's really why this all happened. It changed the train's electrical capacity."

"It doesn't matter." Mifuyu looked worried. "We can't just leave things the way they are. At this rate, not only will the high school division be destroyed, but the spirit will move on to dismantle the rest of the campus."

"Well, there is a way to set things right," the Professor said, "but it's extremely risky." He pulled a letter from his desk. "It just so happens that we're having a specialist brought to CLAMP School to deal with this catastrophe."

"A specialist?" Mifuyu asked.

"Yes. This fellow is sort of an exorcist who travels all over Japan, getting rid of evil spirits."

"Evil spirits—that doesn't sound good," Koji mumbled after a large gasp.

"Ghosts, who among all the ancient spirits, wreak havoc on the living world and all its creatures. Apparently there are a lot more of them than most people realize," the Professor concluded.

BOOM.

A tremor shook the room.

"Oh, no! The Subway Monster must have reached this part of the university!"

"We have no choice," Yuki declared. "We have to buy the exorcist time and hold the demon at bay until he arrives."

"Okay!" the Association shouted in unison.

"C'mon, Koji, let's go." Mifuyu and Yuki darted from the room, heading off in separate directions.

Koji lingered behind. Something still worried him, but he knew he was needed and had to act.

I just hope nothing terrible happens to CLAMP School. It's already suffered enough.

A Gift from the Past

Once upon a time, two shooting stars hurtled through the night sky, witnessed by no one. As if locked in an intergalactic race, they flew to separate points of the earth. One fell into a quiet forested area of eastern Tokyo; the other tumbled into an immense circular-shaped campus city near Tokyo Bay.

The end of the race was met with silence.

Unbeknownst to all, this day marked the birth of something monumental. The day felt unusually idyllic; one could almost feel the footsteps of summer drawing near.

"Our new mission is to investigate the so-called Genbu Park Monster," declared Yuki, the renowned Class A student.

The self-proclaimed "actress of tomorrow," affectionately known as Yuki Ajiadou, twirled around in his new spring-season school uniform, after running his hands through that pride-and-joy hair of his. Eyes aflame from the midday glow, he struck one final, fabulously seductive pose for his audience.

"You all heard about it, right? About the mysterious creature in the artificial pond over in the kindergarten division?"

"Yeah, the way I heard it, it sounded almost like the Loch Ness Monster or something." Mifuyu Mizukagami answered happily, rocking back and forth in her chair. She was a young girl in her third year of high school, assigned to Class Z. She always had a Japanese sword strapped to her back. "According to people who've seen it, this thing swims back and forth in the water, but they can't make out any details. . . . They just see three little humps sticking out of the lake."

"Nuh-uh!" exclaimed Koji Takamura, a Class A grade-schooler sitting next to Mifuyu and looking as handsome as ever in his shorts and suspenders. "The story I heard was that this monster is totally *huge,* and when the moon is full, it jumps in the air like a fish," he said, his suspenders falling down from all the excitement.

"You don't say," Mifuyu said. "If these witnesses were talking to *you,* it's a pretty safe bet they were mistaken."

Mifuyu's dismissive comment irritated Koji. "Yeah, I *do* say," he shot back. "What else could it be? I talked to the Student Body Executive Committee, and they said there aren't any fish that size in Genbu Park, so there's nothing to confuse it with. They did have a theory that one of the black carp might've mutated, but that's about as likely as your *Nessie.*"

"The pond in Genbu Park is emptied out completely at least once a year so that it can be cleaned. It messes with the

environment of the lake, so the council's theory makes sense," commented Takayuki Usagiya, a Class B student, responsible for all the Association's accounts as well as the invaluable task of supplying snacks for meetings. In many ways, he was the true leader of the Association, and when he spoke seriously, he would remove his glasses and wipe the sweat from the earpieces with a cloth. "The Genbu Park pond is a multipurpose reservoir the school built to enhance its study of nature. The possibility of an organism unknown to the student body getting into the water is almost nil."

"True, but after heavy rains, there have been cases of frogs and lungfish migrating to the pond," added Rion Ibuki, a Class C middle-schooler. "Quite a while ago, a lot of people saw this large group of frogs there that had been bred in the nature preserve, and the lungfish that had escaped from the Biology Department aquarium. They ended up in Genbu Park on their search for a new habitat," she concluded, her two full-bodied ponytails bouncing as if to punctuate her point.

Takayuki rested his head on his hands. "Well, I didn't say there was *no* possibility, just that it was slight."

These days, it seemed, anything could happen. Besides, CLAMP School was the type of place where you never knew what each day would bring. It was, after all, a land of adventure, intrigue—and of course—the supernatural.

"All good points, but this is reclaimed land, and it wouldn't be the first time something out of place turned up," Yuki chimed in. It was no surprise that he had something provocative to say. "There have been mummies and other artifacts, and even a spirit that wanted to become human.

"Anyway, our assignment is to simply confirm whatever facts we can confirm. If there really is a monster, only then will our mission turn to its capture. The annual pond cleaning is just around the corner, so time is of the essence."

Yuki looked around the room, sizing up his fellow Association members.

"Since none of you is likely to volunteer for the first stakeout, I suggest we draw straws."

Kyoko Karyuin, employed at the Nanigashi Bank, was the former Chairman of the Supernatural Phenomena Research Association, whose objective was to unravel the various strange and supernatural incidents that occurred, yet went unexplained, at CLAMP School. Also, their existence was still not officially recognized by the school administration, though they had evolved some—they used to be more of a Spooks and Specters Appreciation Society than a true Organization.

Presently, the Association was led by Yuki Ajiadou, who was hand-selected by the original Chairman as her successor. Since taking command, Yuki has strived to advance the Association to recognized Club status. To prove the group's usefulness, he kept his eyes and ears open day and night for incidents to investigate.

Yuki and the other four members—all of them usually dragged around by their leader, rather than truly following him willingly—were specially suited to be part of a collective with a name like the Supernatural Phenomena Research Association.

Each of them possessed supernatural abilities. Some could even be called superhuman.

Yuki, for instance, had the power of teleportation. It should be noted that this could be triggered only when he leapt from a height of at least forty centimeters.

Mifuyu was a master of the ancient martial arts. Perhaps due to her focus on the physical at a young age, she was a little shortchanged in the intellectual department.

Koji was the heir to the master Sengoku ninja family. The Takamura clan was famous across Japan. However, because of certain physical limitations, Koji was not so adept at the more intensive athletic arts.

Takayuki always traveled with a special servant—a former maid of his family's who was now a ghost. Her name was Koizumi, and she had served his household for several generations. Koizumi's tasks ranged anywhere from basic household chores to secret missions, all of which she completed with great finesse. However, because Koizumi was born centuries before, modern technology absolutely baffled her.

Rion was the granddaughter of a Shinto priestess and had inherited powerful spiritual abilities. Unfortunately, her *social* abilities left a little something to be desired.

So, ever since Yuki had assumed command, the Supernatural Phenomena Research Association had become a treasure trove of extraordinary talents. With these resources, the quintet had succeeded in solving a variety of unusual cases.

However, although they had gathered a small number of fans, their efforts were usually for naught. Their Association was consistently denied a Club ranking—and for no other reason than that their work invariably concluded without producing substantial proof of what had occurred.

XOXO

Oh, mannnn . . . why do I have to be first?

As the sun slowly dropped from the sky off to the west, casting its last red embers over the lonely pond, Koji nibbled on the grape bread he had brought for lunch. He was completely alone, so no one was around to hear him curse his usual bad fortune.

Ajiadou-senpai always says the same thing. That the last person to go has lady luck on his side. So why does he always make me draw the bum straw first?

That's what he meant by bad fortune. Always first to draw, always the shortest straw.

There's no such thing as monsters, anyway! Okay, I can't say that for sure, but there's no way that something like that could live in some stupid man-made pond. It's too ridiculous.

Mumbling on, Koji scratched his cheekbones—the ones that made him so famous among the co-eds—and stared blankly at the water. There was nothing to do but wait it out. He pressed his back against a large tree at the foot of the pond, and stretched.

Might as well get comfortable.

Ten minutes passed.

Twenty.

Time sort of flew by. Kind of like a sick bumblebee.

Over by the low bridge on the far end of the water, two duck-shaped boats, the kind built to hold two people, rocked quietly, bumping their noses against each other.

Maybe I should just go home. Not like anyone would know.

But before he could complete his escape plan, a small shadow appeared over the pond.

Huh?

A diminutive figure wearing a kindergarten uniform—a glorified smock, really—with a tartan skirt peeking out from under its hem was standing on the shore.

It's a girl.

The little girl apparently took no notice of the boy watching her. She stood perfectly still and stared at the rippling water.

Her hair was straight and very long, hanging down to just below the edge of her skirt, where it was tied off with a tiny ribbon. She held her hands, like maple leaf *manju* (a sweet Japanese confection made in the shape of a maple leaf), tight to her breast, while her slender fingers moved wildly, as if they had a mind of their own.

Koji realized that he was staring.

Her ethereal beauty struck him in his chest, just left of center, not unlike the crush he had on Koizumi. Of course, in that case, once he had found out she was a ghost, he was absolutely heartbroken.

"—ton." The girl's lips barely quivered. The sound struggled to travel across the park.

. . . hmm?

Koji leaned in to listen.

But he was too late. She spoke no further.

The girl turned on her heels, and just as she had appeared, she disappeared.

It all happened so quickly, Koji didn't know what to do. It was almost like he was paralyzed by his own dull wits.

The silence returned.

She was kind of cute, wasn't she? I wonder what she was doing out here at this hour?

KRSSSH.

A creepy new sound jolted Koji out of his lovesick reverie.
What the—?

The girl had returned with a heavy-looking tank she had dragged to the edge of the pond. The tank was the kind that people used to store heating oil during the winter—you know, square polypropylene—and it was about half the girl's size.

How could that tiny girl have gotten something so unwieldy all the way here? Hauling to the bank of the pond had probably taken every ounce of strength she had. And the weird noise he'd heard must've been her shoving the thing toward the pond. Once she got it as close to the water as possible, she used both her tiny hands to turn it onto its side, still not opening the lid to reveal what was inside.

The girl reached into her uniform pocket and pulled out something wrapped in purple paper. Kneeling over, she unwrapped it, and Koji now saw that there were actually two objects in there. She knocked them together, making a clicking noise.

What is she doing?

Koji smelled something. It was so noxious, it actually made his nose burn. If something could *smell* dangerous, this did.

I know that smell . . . it's gasoline.

CLICK.

Koji's ninja instincts sharpened. He knew that sound. The girl was hitting stones together, trying to get sparks to start a fire.

"Watch out!" Koji was rocked to his bones as a huge explosion shook the park.

"Aaaaaaah!"

Koji felt like he had been pushed through time, only to emerge a split-second later to find the girl in his arms, her scream piercing his eardrums.

In the instant between the spark being struck and the explosion, Koji had sprung into action, dashing like a lightning bolt to grab the girl and bring her to safety.

Koji looked back over his shoulder and saw the plastic tank she had struggled to bring to the water melting in the heat of the fire. Its contents had ignited.

"Wow . . ."

Koji stood there, soaked in cold sweat. He took the girl's hand and helped her to her feet.

"Why on earth would you mess around with something like that?" He didn't even try to mask the anger in his voice. He knew that if he had hesitated for the slightest instant, she would have been engulfed in the flame, possibly burned to death.

The girl opened her mouth, as if she were about to speak—but seeing the rage in Koji's eyes, she turned away. The girl tightened her lips shut, and said nothing.

Koji sighed.

Maybe I shouldn't have yelled at her like that. . . . She's scared, too.

He knelt in front of her and began brushing the dirt off her uniform. His hands moved gently across the fabric.

He let the rhythm of the dusting calm him, and he channeled that calm into his voice. "Gasoline is a pretty effective fuel. It combusts in a car engine over and over, lifting several heavy pistons. If you burn too much of it all at once, though, the way you just did, it explodes. It's extremely destructive. Do you understand?"

Koji thought he was being exceptionally rational and reasonable in his explanation.

The girl didn't respond at all. Fear still colored her face.

He could only hope that she was scared because she had finally grasped the seriousness of her actions and the magnitude of the event. Except his words hadn't calmed her. They'd only freaked her out more, to the point where she was too frozen to speak.

Gahhh . . . at this rate, she'll never tell me anything.

Koji figured it was time to let the subject rest . . . at least for a bit.

Since she isn't injured, I can afford to wait until she's gotten herself together to question her. For now, I should make sure the fire is contained and take her back to the kindergarten.

With his course of action decided, he spoke again. "Well, as long as you realize what you were messing with . . . wait right here. I'm going to clean this mess up, then I'll be right back."

He gave her one last look, and left her side.

He hadn't seen that someone more ominous was approaching.

"So you've finally gone and done it, eh? You've intentionally destroyed a major chunk of school property." The voice came from behind his back, and even though he couldn't see its owner, Koji was pretty sure he recognized it.

"My stars! I always knew it would come to this someday, but I never guessed it would be the pond that would suffer the consequences. And don't tell me this was 'all in the name of research,' because I won't buy it this time."

"Ugh! You're with the Lifestyle-Monitoring Committee, aren't you . . . ?"

Sure enough, standing before them was a low-level member of the Lifestyle-Monitoring Committee, whose members didn't think too highly of the Supernatural Phenomena Research Association. To be quite honest, the two groups were rivals, each seeing the other as a royal nuisance. This particular member—Taro Ryugasaki, a second-year high school student—seemed to have a particular problem with Koji.

"I'll give you a chance to explain yourself," he said. "How I choose to report this incident to the Student Body Executive Committee will depend entirely on what kind of excuse you can manufacture.

"After all, this looks to me like an open act of aggression against CLAMP School."

"N-n-now, w-wait just a minute!"

Koji didn't like being accused, especially in such a patronizing manner. It was as if Taro had already decided that he was guilty, regardless of what Koji had to say.

(Anyone hear of innocent until proven guilty? Dang.)

"I didn't commit arson!" Koji desperately defended himself. "It wasn't me! I even have a witness!"

"Oh, really?" Taro's laugh smacked of self-satisfaction. "Where is this *supposed* witness?"

"Right there," Koji said.

He turned to point at the girl.

"W-what?"

She wasn't there. Nor was there even a hint that she had ever been. Not even a stray hair had been left behind.

"Hold on just a second . . ."

"Hold on to what?" Taro chuckled. "I don't see any witness. Is this person invisible? I bet he or she is just as transparent as your lies."

(There goes that patronizing tone again.)

Taro puffed out his chest, deriving way too much satisfaction from the confrontation. He delivered yet another blow to Koji.

"I ran over here as soon as I saw the flames, and you were the only person in the park. Your defense is pathetic, even for *you!*"

"No, but . . ." Koji protested, ". . . that's not true . . . there was a girl, a kindergartner, who was here just before you showed up. . . ."

Koji tried pleading his case, though in truth he couldn't see the use. The girl was gone. She must have dashed off, maybe hidden in the trees once he had turned away. It seemed like a losing battle.

"You don't sound like even *you* believe your excuse, so why should anyone else?" Taro continued in his disapproving tone. "Keep lying all you want. It will only make you look worse. I'm going to bring this up with the Committee, and they'll hear your pathetic plea then. Now, come with me."

"But . . . uh . . ."

Koji had no choice. Taro dragged him from the park. Nearly two hours of questioning loomed ahead of him.

SPLASH.

As the pair exited, neither of them noticed that something had caused a tiny splash on the surface of Genbu Park Pond.

"This is a problem . . ." assessed Takayuki.

The Association had called an emergency meeting. It had been awhile since the members had gathered in such terrible spirits. Their concern was evident, but Koji looked the worst.

"I'm sorry," he whimpered. "I never thought something like this would happen."

Takayuki met Koji's lethargy with folded arms and a stern resolve. "Don't be silly. It's not your fault. We just have to prove them wrong and prove your innocence."

"But of all the things that could happen," Yuki said worriedly, "you had to get caught by someone from the Lifestyle-Monitoring Committee."

"Well, no sense fussing about that, 'cause caught is caught. . . . It's not something that would have been erased by him *not* being caught." Rion had intended to follow through in Koji's defense, but hadn't planned that it wouldn't make sense.

"Hmmm . . ." Mifuyu had been listening intently, displaying an uncharacteristic seriousness. In her time with the Supernatural Phenomena Research Association, she had seen many instances where the very existence of the Association had been threatened, and each time, it had made her sad.

To everyone's dismay, the Lifestyle-Monitoring Committee pushed its accusation of arson against Koji forward, releasing the following statement:

If evidence proving Koji's innocence is not presented to the Student Body Executive Committee in three days' time, the Supernatural Phenomena Research Association will be officially terminated— with prejudice.

Of course, this surprised no one in the Association. None of them would have expected Miharu Takanashi, the Chairman of the Lifestyle-Monitoring Committee, to rule any differently. She detested the Association.

"So, not only did they reduce us to a 'minor get-together,' " Mifuyu mumbled dejectedly, "they're actually threatening to make us even *more* unofficial than we are now. How much lower can we get?"

"Don't talk like that, Mifuyu," Koji said. "You're going to jinx us." It was a half-hearted protest. He couldn't muster much more.

Although it was he who had kinda sorta gotten the group into this mess, he still didn't believe it could be as bad as it was. The thought of not having the Association to turn to anymore was unacceptable.

"Come on, guys, there's still hope," Yuki said. "We just have to find the girl who really did this, and she can clear it all up. Koji, do you have any leads on her?"

"I found this at the scene." Koji drew a purple cloth out of his pocket. "The rocks the girl used to start the fire had been wrapped in it."

Takayuki spread out the cloth and lifted it to his face.

"Oh . . . !" Rion exclaimed. "Usagiya-senpai, there's some kind of pattern printed on the back."

He flipped the cloth over.

Rion was right. There, imprinted on the fabric, was a large, three-leafed hollyhock design. It reminded him of the kind he'd seen in old samurai dramas.

"It looks like a family crest."

"If that's true, then she could be the daughter of an old family. The crest is very impressive." Mifuyu's admiration was evident. As a descendent of a well-respected family herself, she knew firsthand the significance of such symbols.

"Okay, then," Takayuki said, standing up. "This is the key to finding her. Figure out the family name, find the daughter."

"But Senpai . . . how—?"

"Simple. I'm going to look through the student directory on the computer. I think there's a database of family crests in the public files."

Takayuki ran down the stairs two at a time.

"Here it is. I've got it!" Digging through the library's computers in the student body hall, using the CLAMP School internal search engine, Takayuki found what he was looking for. He smiled to himself, pleased at such a fruitful investigation.

"This is it. Kindergartner—Sakiko Hoshinosuka. She's a perfect match for the physical description Koji gave us."

He dragged her ID photo to the right side of the monitor and switched it over to the 360-degree scan that the school took of all its students. Takayuki hurriedly scribbled all the information about her into his student handbook.

"That's her. Her name is Sakiko-chan."

Koji took the photocopy from Takayuki's hand. "It sure is," he said. "A dead ringer. Is this her address? Wow. Tokyo West Region Interior S City, Hoshinosuka Village! She lives really far away from the school."

"Yeah," Takayuki confirmed. "She commutes here every day by *helicopter*. Her parents are big real-estate moguls who deal in forest land."

Koji breathed a sigh of relief; however, Yuki realized there was no time to rest. They couldn't afford to relax. His mind went into hyper drive, formulating a plan of action.

"First," he said, "we'll go to the entrance of the kindergarten division and wait for her to show up. It's not even four o'clock yet, so there's a good chance she hasn't left for home. Given your foot speed, you should be able to get across campus in a matter of minutes, Koji."

"Huh? I doubt he can get there as fast as you when you teleport, Senpai!" Rion said.

Yuki had already thought of that. "True, but I've never met Sakiko-chan, and she might be suspicious of some guy she's never seen before popping up out of nowhere. She's at least somewhat familiar with Koji, and she may be more willing to hear our case if he's the one doing the talking."

Takayuki reluctantly agreed. "He has a point." But he couldn't help thinking this was yet another case of Yuki sloughing the dirty work off onto others.

"Okay, then. We have to get her cooperation quickly. We need her to go to the Student Body Executive Committee as soon as possible. Strike while the iron's hot, Koji! Go work your magic!"

Koji didn't move.

"What's the matter?"

"If you don't mind, I'd like to handle this on my own. *All* of this, not just Sakiko-chan."

"What?"

The other kids looked at Koji as if he were speaking in tongues.

"Why?"

"What on earth for?"

"Well . . ." he said slowly, choosing his words carefully, ". . . if we dragged her in front of the Student Body Executive Committee without getting to the bottom of the story ourselves, I might be off the hook, but wouldn't they point the finger at her instead?"

"Of course they would," Yuki answered flatly. "She did it."

"Maybe . . . but I think she must have had a reason for doing what she did. . . . I mean, she went through the trouble of bringing the tank of gasoline; she had it in her head that she was going to set the pond on fire."

"Duh! That's exactly why we need to turn her in. She's got some serious explaining to do."

The group glared at Koji, but his face remained stony.

"But maybe—"

Mifuyu held up her hand, stopping him mid-sentence. "Koji-kun, is there something special about this girl? You act like you don't think she should have to pay for her crime."

"*Exactly!*"

The word popped out before Koji even had a chance to consider what he was saying. And once it did, it uncorked the rest.

"It's not right. She's still only in kindergarten, and she's just a kid. If she gets sent up the river for this, she may never come back down. . . . I can't explain why, but I just *know* that's something we can't let happen."

Rion threw up her hands. "So, it's better you take the rap for burning up the park, so she can continue to cause trouble?"

"No," Takayuki said. "Let him do as he likes. It's Koji's case." Takayuki moved closer to Koji, with only about a foot separating them. "Just remember, you have *only three days*. After that, if you don't have your explanation, we give up the girl."

"Thank you."

Koji quickly bowed his head, and then dashed like the wind to go find his quarry.

"Senpai!" Rion shouted. "How could you do that? Are you serious? If he doesn't pull this off, Koji-kun is going to get convicted, and it'll all be over for him."

Takayuki removed his glasses and wiped away the sweat. "What can we do?" he asked, his expression pained. "Koji's mind is made up."

"Boy, oh boy." Yuki let out a heavy sigh and dropped down into one of the metal chairs in the room. "I hope the kid is right."

Rion nervously rocked back and forth on the balls of her feet. She still wasn't sure this was a good idea.

ࣩ ࣩ

"Say, don't you think the Back Hill is looking pretty desolate these days?"

The afternoon sky was pure blue. A grade school girl and her friend sat beneath it, reclining on the hill and eating a delicious picnic lunch.

"Really?" the friend asked, her mouth packed with jam-filled buns. "I guess I hadn't noticed."

The Back Hill was another name for the man-made Hillside Park, built specifically to lend terrain of the grade school campus some variety. It was erected on the opposite side of Genbu Park, bordering the kindergarten campus with only a little over two kilometers between them.

"It's strange," the first girl said. "This place used to be blooming with daisies, but now there isn't a single flower in sight. Even the grass looks dried out. Summer is just around the corner. The plants should be colorful and alive."

"You don't say?" Her friend didn't seem to mind at all. The food she was munching on was more important than the foliage around her. "You're thinking too much. The grass is probably just letting some other plants take over or something. You said it yourself: It's practically the change of the seasons."

"I bet it's always like this at this time of year."

"I wonder . . ."

Offering a French roll to her friend, the girl looked around the hillside with a sense of unease.

After class, near the edge of the Genbu Park Pond, an early summer gust blew past a solitary kindergarten girl. Her long hair was tied with a small ribbon.

As she approached the large tree growing on the pond's bank, she looked down at the soil and quietly closed her eyes. And then, with a voice as soft as the wind in her hair, she spoke.

"I'm sorry."

"I knew you would come here," echoed a voice from the darkness.

She hadn't seen anyone when she had arrived, so the voice raining down from above was startling, to say the least.

A small figure, cloaked so deeply in shadow it could have been mistaken for the shadow itself, swung out of the tree and landed on its feet in front of her.

"You fell for the Takamura Clan tree-disguise technique," Koji said. "I knew you'd come back here, so it was just a matter of waiting it out."

A barely audible *"uh . . . uh . . ."* managed to escape from her lips.

The girl was panicking. Her hands were shaking, her throat choking on her words. She shifted her weight onto a single heel and twisted herself around, preparing to run.

"Hey, wait!" Koji said as he tried to grab her, his fingers grasping at air. "Don't run away! I'm not here to turn you in!"

The girl paused.

"I'm not mad about the whole fire thing from yesterday. I was more worried about you than anything. You totally disappeared. It took a lot of effort to find you."

Slowly, Sakiko turned back around to face him. Her eyes were wide with fear, but gentle. They were dark, and Koji felt like they were swallowing him whole.

She looked like a little deer that had found itself face-to-face with a hunter.

Koji felt tenseness grip his back.

"If you're afraid of me, it's okay. I won't come any closer . . . but I *have* to talk to you. I need to know why you did what you did yesterday. And why you ran away. That's all I ask."

M-maybe I should smile to try to show her she can trust me?

Koji told his mouth to smile, but the best it could come up with was a sort of awkward half-grin. He hoped that his intentions would be clear regardless, and maybe they were, because she no longer looked like she intended to run. There was still some hesitation to her movements, but finally she spoke.

"You . . . you won't tell anyone?"

"I already said—"

"No, not that I did it. You won't tell anyone the *reason?*"

"Oh, no. I mean, yes. That is, I won't tell anyone. I promise."

Koji shook his head vigorously. When words failed, there were still gestures.

Again, whatever his fumblings, the meaning got through. Sakiko visibly eased up, slowly inching toward him.

"He's in the pond," she said.

"Huh?"

"My . . . Zetton."

Koji couldn't believe it. *She didn't just say . . . ?*

"Zetton? You mean . . . *that* Zetton?"

It seemed even more unbelievable now that he'd repeated it. "You mean, the ultimate monster, the one that defeated Ultraman in the very last episode?"

He might have only been twelve, but Koji knew his vintage sci-fi television shows very well.

Sakiko, on the other hand, did not. She cocked her head to one side and said, "I don't know. He just keeps crying, 'Zetton, Zetton,' and so I decided that was his name. Zetton."

"Uh-oh."

It was even worse than Koji had imagined. "B-but is there really an animal that makes a sound like that? I've heard that a screech owl makes a noise that sounds like *bupposo*, which is why people called the owls Bupposos, so—"

"There *is* a creature that says 'Zetton,' " Sakiko said. "I found him by my house."

Timidly, Sakiko began to tell the story of how she first encountered Zetton.

Oh! A falling star . . .

Peering at the clear, cloudless night sky from her window, Sakiko saw a streak of light shoot across the sky's face. Without realizing, she started to clap with joy.

I hope I can meet an animal friend. I hope I can meet an animal friend. I hope I can meet an animal friend. . . .

"You know that's not possible, Sakiko. You know your father doesn't like animals."

"But . . . Mother!"

"I'm sorry, but you're going to have to give up on that wish. If you try to get a dog or cat, your father will have a heart attack. Fish and birds are out of the question, too. He'll just fry them up and eat them."

Sakiko was tired of all of her friends having pets to play with while she had none. So she had been wishing on a star every night, hoping that she could meet some sweet animal and befriend it. She had heard that if you repeated your wish three times when you saw a falling star, then the wish would come true.

I wonder if the star heard me this time.

WHOOOOOOSH.

Oh!

Normally, the star fell out of sight and was instantly gone. Not this time.

Oh . . . oh, my . . .

It was heading straight for the woods next to Sakiko's house, cutting a direct path into the trees.

Whoa!

BOOM!

There was a heavy crash, heavier than the sound you'd hear if you dropped a big book onto a wooden floor. It shook the whole area.

"What was that?!"

Below her window, a handful of servants from the house were running about, trying to find out what happened. Not wanting to be left out—especially since she was the only one with any real inkling of what had occurred—Sakiko jumped into her shoes and ran downstairs, heading outside.

She made a beeline for the woods.

She didn't even think about it. She felt compelled to go in that direction.

"Zet . . . ton."

Yikes.

The voice came out of the shrubbery. She couldn't tell from where.

Uh . . .

Sakiko pulled back the bushes, and there it was.

"Zet . . . ton."

The creature was trying to extract itself from a transparent egg-like shell. It looked weakly at Sakiko.

Its voice sounded strained as it cried out its name a third time.

"I took Zetton home with me, and I kept him hidden from my parents while he grew."

Koji looked like he had seen a ghost. He hadn't expected such a wild tale from the girl.

"He was so small, he fit inside my hand," she continued, "so it wasn't as difficult as it sounds. He was filthy, so I filled up a washbowl with some well water. He swam around it like he was some kind of fish. He liked it so much, the washbowl became his home."

"Oh, so he's a water creature."

"Kinda. But he actually likes fire more."

"Huh?" Koji had never heard of a creature that liked fire. "What do you mean?"

"It's weird . . . I didn't know what kind of food he ate. I tried feeding him milk and bread and lots of stuff we had around the house, but he didn't want any of it. It just so happened he was near me one day when I was making a fire—"

"Uh-huh."

❧ ☙

". . . Oh, no! *Zetton!*"

The tiny creature had somehow wrenched himself out of the washbowl and was zipping toward the fire.

"How—?"

Sakiko tried to stop him, afraid that the flames would burn him to a crisp.

But Zetton trotted up to the fire and began deeply breathing it in . . .

"He inhaled the fire?!"

"Uh-huh."

Koji's eyes were so wide, he thought they were going to fall out of their sockets.

Sakiko, on the other hand, couldn't have been more matter-of-fact, as if what she was saying were the most natural thing in the world.

"He stayed by the fire for a bit, and then I guess he got full. He had sucked up so much of it, he had nearly put the fire out. As soon as he was done, he curled up and went right to sleep. It was the cutest thing I'd ever seen."

Remembering the moment made Sakiko smile. It was the first time Koji had seen her be anything but afraid.

"After that, I'd make him a fire every day. I had to be careful not to be caught, so I used a lot of different things to burn, at a lot of different places. My little guy *had* to eat."

"B-but what kind of animal can actually eat *fire?*"

The only creature Koji could think of that was similar to the one in Sakiko's story was Nanigashi, a monster that looked kind of like a turtle. He'd seen it in a movie—which meant it was *imaginary*. There weren't any fire-eating animals in the *real* world.

"Well, this kind can. I fed him fire every day."

Koji swallowed hard. *There's more to this story?*

"But he got too big. Every time he had some fire, he would grow. It was a little more each time, sometimes a whole centimeter with a single breath. In about a month, he was bigger than most cats. A few weeks, later he was bigger than any of my friends' dogs.

"He outgrew the washbowl in about two weeks. I had to start keeping him in the bathtub. Our house is so big, we each have our own bathroom, so it was safe . . . until even the bathtub got too small. I didn't know where else Zetton could go without my mom finding him."

"I see," Koji said, "so you brought him to Genbu Park and set him free in the pond, is that it?"

Koji wondered how Sakiko could sneak something like that onto campus and into the park, but he was terrified to think of what the answer might be. It was already too wild for words.

The story was too incredible to be a lie. Sakiko had to be telling the truth.

It all makes sense. The rumors about the monster in the lake started about the same time Sakiko-chan released Zetton into it. And if what Sakiko-chan said about her parents banning pets is true, it makes sense that she didn't want to talk about it. And the fire wasn't meant to be destructive. The opposite, in fact.

"Let me guess . . . once you let Zetton go, you couldn't find him again."

"Y-yeah." Sakiko nodded sadly.

It was just as Koji had suspected. If the creature had spent most of his time in the water, which would explain why none of the other students had ever really *seen* him, but only caught glimpses.

Koji sighed.

"Even if you meant well, it was dangerous for you to start that fire here," he said. "And you didn't know if Zetton would even show up, so it could've been a big risk for nothing. Did you ever stop to think there might be a reason why he's hiding?"

Sakiko looked at him as her cheeks puffed out and her bottom lip quivered. Tears started to well up in her eyes, so she bit her lip to keep from crying. It didn't work.

"Has Zetton forgotten about me already?"

"No!" Koji protested. "That can't be true. There's no way that Zetton could forget about you, Sakiko-chan. I'm sure there's a perfectly logical explanation."

Koji had no basis for what he was saying. But Sakiko needed to hear it, so he said it with as much conviction as he could muster.

It didn't do any good. Sakiko continued to cry.

Oh, man. I'm no good when it comes to girls who cry. What should I do . . . ? Oh, I know.

"Sakiko-chan," Koji said, "I'll find Zetton for you."

"What . . . ?" Sakiko stared at him through glistening, tear-soaked eyes. "You mean it?"

She wiped her nose. Her cheeks were flushed from crying so hard.

"I do. I have some senpais that are pretty keen at this sort of thing, and together, we can find *anything*. So, don't worry. Leave everything to me."

Koji thumped his chest.

Sure, he was blustering, but he just couldn't bear seeing such an adorable girl in tears.

Sakiko began to smile, just a little bit, and that made it all worth it.

Koji felt his own cheeks heat up with a deep blush.

The night that followed started off peacefully enough.

RUMBLE.

"Hmmm . . . ?"

RUMBLE. RUMBLE. RUMBLE.

"Eeeee!"

"W-what's going on?"

Two high schoolers had thought the empty park would be a nice, tranquil spot for a date. But now they were cowering in the darkness as the ground trembled beneath them.

"It's an earthquake!"

"I-I think it's over, though."

As the rumbling subsided, the two could only stand there in shock.

Earthquakes were a rare occurrence at CLAMP School. The campus grounds were outfitted with tremor-absorbing mechanisms whose performance had been nearly perfect. The mechanisms had been able to neutralize just about every earthquake that hit Japan since they were built.

This was the first time the young lovers had felt an earthquake of any kind at the school.

"It's, like, a bad omen or something. We should get out of here."

The couple had been strolling blissfully through the artificial area of the grade school park, more commonly known as the Back Hill. But all thoughts of a romantic evening disappeared as they ran back to their dorms as fast as their legs would carry them.

Following the earthquake at the Back Hill, something rose to the surface of the Genbu Park Pond.

After a moment of exposing itself to the fresh air, it submerged again.

"If that's true, then this is going to be some fantastic case. . . ."

The way Takayuki was murmuring, it wasn't clear if he were speaking to anyone else, or just to himself.

"I believe Sakiko-chan," Koji said, looking intently into the faces of his fellow Association members. "Zetton really *is* in that pond.

"She wasn't lying to me. Don't you remember what Karyuin-senpai told us? She said that if we were convinced a witness wasn't lying, then no matter how unbelievable their story might be, we must accept the possibility that it really happened and isn't just a figment of their imagination. It's our job as members of this Association to find out for sure."

"But . . ." Rion had a worried look on her face. "Have you seriously considered what happens if you take the blame for setting that blaze?"

It was the following day, and Koji was using the early morning meeting to fill his friends in on his conversation with Sakiko. He was mindful of his promise to her, and he told his associates that they were burdened by the same vow—that they could never speak a word of her tale to *anyone*.

The story had excited the others, but just as much over their concern that it would be the ruin of Koji as for the notion that a creature like Zetton existed.

"I still don't know what I am going to do about the Lifestyle-Monitoring Committee," Koji said. The tone of his voice didn't exactly scream confidence. "If we can find Zetton . . . well, I feel bad for Sakiko-chan, but I'll be able to prove my innocence.

"Hopefully she'll understand. It would be good for her, too, because if we can put the blame on Zetton, then Sakiko-chan is cleared of the crime, as well."

"I hope you're right," Rion grumbled.

"Regardless, our mission is to find Zetton, and we have a strict forty-eight-hour deadline. We need to hurry."

"Okay, let's do it!" Mifuyu exclaimed.

Koji reached his hand inside his pocket. Grasping a hard metal object, he pulled it out.

"If you're going to look for Zetton, you should take this."

"What is it?"

"It was lying there . . . next to Zetton . . . when he landed."

He held out his hand. On his open palm lay a shiny silver plate.

Sakiko-chan, I'll find Zetton for you. . . . I have some senpais that are pretty keen at this sort of thing, and together, we can find anything.

Koji realized something. He looked around the room, confused. "Hey . . . I thought something was missing here. Where's Yuki-senpai?"

They met at the same time and place every day, so it was strange not to see Chairman Yuki there.

Takayuki cleared his throat. "Oh, yeah . . . Yuki-chan," he said. "He's in supplementary classes."

"Supplementary classes?" It almost seemed more incredible to Koji than the story Sakiko had told him. "How could that be? Ajiadou-senpai is smarter than anyone. Why would he have to take supplementary classes?"

It really didn't make sense.

Sure, Yuki was a strange student, one who believed he was the embodiment of the heart and soul of womankind, but he was certifiably brilliant. Many often wondered why he hadn't been selected as a scholarship student for Class Z. His intelligence was of a supremely high level.

"Well, you see," Takayuki explained, "given how much time the Chairman puts into his extracurricular activities, lately he hasn't been studying all that much."

"Did his grades go down?"

"Well, in a word . . . yes."

Takayuki was as smart as Yuki, if not smarter, but he also knew full well that studying was key. He was always diligent in both preparing and reviewing the material for his classes.

That any student as smart as Yuki could end up in this situation truly perplexed Koji.

"The Chairman had a field trip to the Back Hill as part of today's agenda, and the class should be getting back soon."

Aghhhh. This is making me so mad.

The steamy weather at the Back Hill was getting on Yuki's nerves. Although the sky was clear and blue, the air was stale and hot. He was clutching grass samples from the day's field studies in his hand.

This is a rotten time of year to be working outdoors. Not to mention, the Association is in a crisis. It's terribly inconvenient. Why do I have to take these stupid classes, anyway? Can't they just trust me when I say I'm smart?

"Pick up the pace, Yuki. If you don't harvest the plant samples assigned to you, you won't receive credit."

The biology teacher was watching Yuki from across the field and showing little sympathy for someone of the Chairman's stature.

"All right already. Sheesh."

Yuki sighed. He squatted down to gather more grass.

What a beast. How could he do this to a girl? My hands and clothes are getting filthy. Just because it's a supplementary class doesn't mean they should force us to do manual labor.

THUNK.

Ugh.

An accident cut off Yuki's train of thought, and the Chairman found himself tumbling down a large hole that had opened up beneath him.

Owwwww . . . what is this?

After landing at the bottom, Yuki noticed a large tunnel ahead of him. It was just about the right size for a single person to crawl through. The best he could guess was that the weight of his squatting body had caused the dirt beneath him to give way, taking him down this connecting tunnel.

Is it a mole trail? No, it's too big for that. It's nearly a meter in diameter. No way a little mole dug that.

Yuki felt himself going into Supernatural-Phenomena-Research-Association mode. His inquisitive instinct was pulsing.

I know. This discovery could be just what we're looking for. If I can solve the puzzle, then I can earn the Association some credibility and keep them from shutting us down. I've got to see where this goes.

Unfortunately for Yuki, he had no idea he had stumbled upon the beginning of even more trouble.

The Professor was baffled.

On his desk sat what appeared to be, at least at first glance, an ordinary silver plate.

It was the mysterious object that Koji had received from Sakiko.

The plate was small, measuring two-by-three centimeters, and Sakiko had retrieved it from around where the creature's capsule (or, was it really an egg?) had touched down.

The Professor had been asked to analyze the object in hopes it would provide a clue as to the creature's origins, or at least help them find where Zetton was now.

But the Professor just stared at the plate and sighed for the millionth time.

"Hmmm . . . as far as its material substance and form, I can probably determine, with a little help from one of the other professors, how it's put together, but when it comes to discovering the hidden meaning behind the plate itself, I have no idea even where to begin."

No matter how many times he looked at it, no matter how many times he studied it, the Professor couldn't come close to fathoming what sort of secrets the plate might be hiding . . . that is, if it hid any secrets at all. If it was just an ordinary metal plate, then he was just making a fool of himself.

There wasn't any type of lettering on the object, no design of any kind. Its surface was completely smooth on both sides. In fact, the only thing peculiar about the plate was the *lack* of scratches and dents on its surface.

Regardless, the Professor had no idea how to unravel the mystery now before him. He wouldn't have even gone this far if it weren't for Yuki, who was making the request. He was a pretty big fan of the Supernatural Phenomena Research Association, and of its Chairman in particular. If Yuki were bringing the challenge, he'd accept it willingly . . . but with his study of the object getting him nowhere, he felt his only available recourse was to sigh (yet again).

A beam of light from the summer sun filtered in through the laboratory window and illuminated the dim room.

"Light, eh? Maybe I should try holding it up to the sun. Perhaps it's secretly transparent . . . except it's a solid piece of metal, so how could it be?"

Despite his doubts, the Professor carried the silver plate to the window; however, because he was so deep in thought, his sense of balance went completely wonky.

(He was goin' down.)

"Whoa!"

SHUNK.

The silver plate slipped from his hand, and as it hit the floor, a small sound—like a beautiful note struck on a tuning fork—reverberated through the lab.

"Oh, bother. They left the plate in my care and I dropped it."

The sunlight hit the plate where it rested on the floor, and when it bounced off the solid disc, a dazzling light spread all across the room.

"Oh, my."

The Professor stared at the refracted light. The sight of it was stunning.

A rectangular reflection appeared on the ceiling, and inside that rectangle, strange letters began to emerge.

The ghostly shapes had a formulaic cast to them, and appeared to spell out a code. But what could it be?

On the previous night, a tall boy in silver-rimmed glasses was bathed in moonlight.

"Are you ready?" he asked the darkness, speaking softly.

"Yes, sir," the darkness replied.

From the shadow of a tree, a small boy emerged. He was dressed in specialized garb, and he moved soundlessly.

"I've got my bamboo snorkel, a mini-searchlight, swim fins, and an airbag. I'm all set for the underwater search."

"Okay, get in the pond while nobody's looking. Be as quiet as a monk, and no sudden movements."

"Yes, sir."

The small boy slid both of his feet into the fins, and began to run briskly—if awkwardly—toward the pond.

"Ngh!"

"What?"

"Ahhhhh!"

Suddenly, a bank of searchlights was switched on, and the entire park lit up bright as day.

"Welly, well, well. I thought you might try something like this. It was a good thing I alerted the Security Committee."

From a platform tucked away behind the searchlights, propped up in the treetops, a woman stepped forward. The searchlights enveloped her from behind.

"Not . . . Miharu Takanashi?!"

Takayuki shielded the light from his eyes with his hands, but a beam managed to make its way between his fingers, bouncing off his silver-rimmed glasses, giving his face an opaque glow.

He was hoping to block out enough light so that he could see who was there.

It *was* Miharu Takanashi, Chairman of the Lifestyle-Monitoring Committee. She was also wearing glasses with lenses as thick as the bottoms of milk bottles. She pushed them up her nose and then released them with an arrogant laugh, assuming a pose of victory. She looked down on Takayuki.

"I knew that you people wouldn't sit quietly and accept your punishment," she said. "So predictable . . . like in a bad detective novel, the criminals return to the scene of their crime. It's a shamefully stupid move for those who think they're so smart. Did you really think you could get away with it?"

Takayuki's pride bristled under the woman's conceited gaze. "So what? If we're to clear our comrade's name, then we're free to investigate the charges. We're students here, and since this is a school matter, we have the freedom to exhaust every available avenue."

"Such optimism. You're right, students *are* free to investigate school matters as much as they like—as long as the students are involved in *legitimate* activities. Involvement in an *illegal* organization is a different story altogether, particularly when the organization's main function is to make trouble. Do you think I'm dumb enough to let such a group have access to a crime scene where they can tamper with evidence to their hearts' content?"

CRIK.

Takayuki gritted his teeth so hard, it could be heard across the park.

Before he knew what was happening, several figures surrounded him. By their uniforms, it was obvious they were part of the Security Committee Miharu had called for backup.

Takayuki was helpless against them.

Except . . .

"Senpai!" Koji called out to his Supernatural Phenomena Research Association colleague from the shadowy spot he'd ducked into when the lights came on. Takayuki was relieved to hear his voice.

"Koji? Where are you?"

"Senpai, take cover!"

POOF.

Takayuki was instantly enshrouded in black smoke.

"What the—? H-how—?"

Miharu's mouth fell open in shock. Her glasses slipped back down her nose.

The security officers tried to wave the smoke away, but as it dissipated, they discovered that Takayuki was no longer behind it.

"No! How could they—? Is this some kind of magic trick?"

Miharu may have *said* these words, but she definitely didn't *believe* that something as ethereal as magic actually existed; her commitment to science was that strong.

But, for once in her life, her beloved science failed her. Takayuki had vanished into thin air, and she had no idea how.

"So, anyway . . . I'm really sorry, Sakiko-chan! I haven't found Zetton yet."

The next day had come all too quickly. Half their time was gone.

Koji barely had enough time to go home and change out of his ninja uniform before returning to CLAMP School. He tried to arrive at his usual time, to give the appearance that nothing was out of the ordinary. After classes, he reconvened with the Association, where heads hung low.

Zetton's owner, the kindergartner from Hoshi Gumi, had come with him. Sakiko was sitting in a chair made of old metal piping. She looked ready to burst into tears. Had her eyes been cast down any further, they'd be resting on the tops of her shoes.

"I couldn't believe it," Takayuki muttered. "I never would have thought they'd be standing guard over Genbu Park."

Takayuki wasn't used to crawling along the ground, so the escape the night before had been an entirely new experience. He suffered scratches all over his body, and when he folded his arms, he could feel the bandages running up and down them. But they didn't hurt nearly as much as the shame he felt standing before the other Association members.

The Association was determined to search for the missing Zetton. Since Sakiko had released him into the Genbu Park Pond, that was the logical place to begin. Fulfilling Sakiko's wish to reunite with her pet was a secondary goal; the mission's real impetus was to clear Koji's name, which Miharu was trying to make impossible for them. She was dedicated to bringing their Association down, and she wasn't going to let a single person near that pond before Koji's deadline was up.

With only a day left, the group was no closer to solving the case than they'd been when they started.

"If we can't find this Zetton by tomorrow after class, the Student Body Executive Committee is going to weigh in on this mess and order our Association to disband. There has to be some way."

Takayuki gritted his teeth again. The sound traveled through the room.

Mifuyu was noticeably distraught. If the oldest member of the Supernatural Phenomena Research Association was so completely freaked out, what chance did they have? She could see it was tearing him up, and it was weighing heavily on the little girl at the center of the maelstrom, too. "Poor Sakiko-chan," she whispered.

Sakiko began to sob. "Zetton must have died. . . . He was all alone at the bottom of the pond, and I . . . I put him there."

"S-Sakiko-chan . . ." Koji rushed to comfort her. "That's not true. You know Zetton is tougher than that. He's alive and well and swimming through the water right now."

"But . . ."

"You can't give up yet, Sakiko-chan. You have to keep hoping until the absolute last moment."

Koji wanted more than anything for her to believe his words.

"Okay," Saikiko said slowly. She nodded. Believing, even for a moment, cheered her up.

Takayuki lifted his face. "Koji's right. Don't give up until it's all over . . . okay?"

Takayuki headed for the door. Mifuyu jumped up and went after him. "What are you going to do?" she asked.

"Let's go see the Professor, the one who's always doing favors for the Chairman. Yesterday I asked him to take a look at the silver plate Sakiko-chan took from the creature's crash site. Maybe he found something," Takayuki answered.

Just days before all this started, during the Subway Monster incident, the Professor had provided the group with all sorts of information. Whenever Takayuki and the others found themselves in a pinch, the Professor's advice equipped them to break through to the other side, and in the case of the Subway Monster, it led to them being able to chase that particular nightmare off the campus.

"Oh! I want to come, too!"

"Me, too!"

Hearing Takayuki's plan, Koji and Sakiko leapt from their chairs.

"By the way," Koji said, as if he had only just thought of it, "does anyone know what the Chairman and Ibuki-senpai are up to?"

This was the second meeting in a row that Chairman Yuki had missed. He was always there, so the absence was unsettling.

Furthermore, the middle school student, Rion, took great pride in her punctuality. It was just as rare for her to miss a meeting as it was for Yuki.

"Oh, Yuki-chan and Rion discovered a new monster," Takayuki explained, "and are hot on its trail."

"Say what?"

"Think of it as a backup plan. If for some reason we're unsuccessful, but they come up with something grand on their end, then the Association's stock will go up."

But by the way he said this, it was clear that Takayuki had his doubts about the plan.

As soon as his friend finished speaking, Koji sighed within his heart.

"Here! Over *here!* This is where I fell in. Do you sense anything strange, Rion-chan?"

Yuki had dragged Rion to the Back Hill, over on the grade school campus. He took her to the hole he had fallen into during his field trip.

"Not really," she replied, timidly. "I'm not picking up any kind of spiritual presence in particular."

"Don't just look for spirits. We don't know what this thing is. Set your radar for fairies, monsters, whatever. If it's got a supernatural pulse, and if science can't figure out what it is, I want you to find it."

"But I can't just . . ." Rion stopped herself. She was embarrassed to admit it, but Yuki was asking for too much. Although her spiritual senses were strong, they weren't all-encompassing. There was a limit to what she could track.

"Well, anyway, take a look at this." Yuki sprinted across the field and began rummaging through the grass. "I found this yesterday and hid it here."

He scooped up a handful of soil, then shoved it aside.

"What's that?" Rion asked, a little surprised.

Yuki had exposed a gaping pit.

"I was digging around and just happened to fall in this hole. Isn't it wild? And look, there's this amazing tunnel at the bottom here."

"You're right . . . wow!"

Rion knelt down and peered inside. The size of the tunnel was impressive, and she was starting to think the Chairman was on to something.

"I've never seen an animal around here large enough to do that, so who knows what's down there?" Yuki was gesturing wildly. "If we can find it and study it, we can show the results to the Student Body Executive Committee and convince them that they need us around."

Yuki puffed up his chest with pride.

Only Rion had other things in mind. . . .

I wonder if these cases are connected? Could Sakiko-chan's Zetton have done this?

She shook her head, disagreeing with herself.

No . . . there's no way. After all, Zetton is an aquatic creature. He lives in the pond at Genbu Park.

And Genbu Park was more than two kilometers away from the Back Hill.

Still, as she examined the tunnel, it did seem to continue on for a long way. The connection with Zetton wasn't entirely *impossible*.

Meanwhile, Takayuki and the others were visiting the research lab in the university section of campus. The Professor had a theory for them, but it wasn't what anyone had expected.

"You're saying that Zetton might be some kind of ancient creature?"

"That's right."

Takayuki, Mifuyu, Koji, and Sakiko gasped in unison. Their eyes grew as wide as the sliver plate in the Professor's hands.

"I found some lettering on the plate. It was a complete accident, but then, that's science for you. I have about half of it translated. Evidently, the beings that produced these markings possess an extremely sophisticated technology."

There was wildness in the Professor's eyes. He seemed intoxicated by his discovery. His sense of excitement only increased as he launched into the story of how he had stumbled on the lettering just that morning.

"That's one tricky plate," Mifuyu said with a laugh.

"I'll read to you what I've translated so far," the Professor said. " 'The roots of calamity Blahbbity Blah Blah.' I don't know what this 'Blahbbity Blah Blah' means, but my best conjecture is that it's some kind of proper noun, like the name of something."

" 'The roots of calamity?' " Koji was starting to look uneasy.

"Professor, you don't suppose that Zetton could be the *root* of this calamity, do you?"

"No way?!" Sakiko ruffled at Takayuki's words.

"Well, I can't really say," the Professor answered. "But let me continue with my translation: 'The roots of calamity Blahbbity Blah Blah. Our world was almost destroyed by the

Bippity Boppity Boo. However, by virtue of great sacrifice, we finally captured it, sealed the wretched thing in a capsule, and ejected it from our land into the great skies.' "

"What?"

" 'As a gift to future generations, in order to prevent further disaster at the hands of the Blahbbity Blah Blah, the havoc it is sure to wreak. . . .' Let's see: 'We shot into space a bio-weapon organism, housed in a separate capsule all its own.' "

"Whaaaaa—?"

"Wait, there's more. . . . Well, according to what I can make out, it appears that a civilization that preceded humankind and lived right here ended up launching two paranormal organisms into outer space."

"In other words . . ." Koji began with much trepidation, "y-you mean the Zetton creature that Sakiko-chan found is one of those two organisms?"

"If what's written here is true, then that's exactly what I mean. Either way, until my colleague figures out the key to translating the rest of these writings, I can't honestly say for sure. We could be misreading the whole thing."

As the Professor's words sank in, the color drained from both Takayuki's and Koji's faces.

If the Professor's translation turned out to be correct, then there was a fifty-percent chance that Zetton was the Blahbbity Blah Blah that might destroy the world.

Sakiko's expression grew dark and she grabbed Mifuyu's hand. They were both on the edge of panic.

XOXO

"Are you ready? 'Cause we need to get moving."

"Are you sure this is safe, Senpai? It's more than a little freaky."

Rion was gripped by a sense of unease, but Yuki was already crouched down in the pit, half in the tunnel and half out.

"I'll be fine," Yuki declared confidently. He lit a torch he had fashioned out of a piece of firewood wrapped with old newspapers. "I'd feel a little better if our leading warrior, Mifuyu-chan, was here, but if worse comes to worst, I can always teleport myself to safety. It's just a matter of side-stepping the danger."

Of course, he had to work around the fact that his powers depended on him making a leap of some height. If they came across any danger, Rion was supposed to yank on the rope tied around Yuki's waist and lift him forty centimeters into the air. Then, once the momentum started, the two of them would teleport straight out of there.

Feeling secure with his plan, Yuki was about to embark on possibly his boldest assignment yet. He was on a mission to smoke out whatever monstrosity was waiting at the other end of this tunnel.

"If it's a big mole or some kind of *tanuki* or something, I'll let you know immediately, Rion-chan. At the slightest hint of danger, haul me out of there."

"O-okay . . ."

The torch caught fire, sizzling and popping as it burned. Yuki blew the smoke back behind him and out of the tunnel.

None of this was making Rion feel any better about what he was about to do.

According to Sakiko, Zetton *liked* fire.

If the creator of the tunnel was in fact Zetton, as she suspected, then wasn't burning fire practically an act of suicide?

I really hope Yuki knows what he's doing.

She stopped.

Something was sparkling. Its glint, which could be seen just beyond the bushes, was distracting.

What's that . . . ?!

She knew she was supposed to be keeping an eye on Yuki, but still, she couldn't shake the feeling that she had to take a closer look at whatever was sparkling so.

In the shrubs she found a small, round object—like a capsule of some kind.

It was broken open, and the trail in the dirt suggested something had crawled out.

How strange.

Rion recalled that Sakiko had told them Zetton had been in some kind of egg-like capsule when she found him.

Oh, my . . . is this . . . ?

"Hey, I have the rest of the translation."

A laid-back lab-coat-wearing man ambled into the room. In contrast to the sober demeanor of the Professor and the Association members, he appeared extremely relaxed. The man obviously hadn't grasped the meaning of the message he'd translated.

"Here you go."

He casually handed a piece of paper to the Professor.

"I gotta tell you, this is some weird stuff you've dug up. You translating some sort of old-school sci-fi novel?"

"I wish that were true." The Professor laughed nervously, hoping a vague answer would do. (apparently it did, because the guy left) He quickly scanned the paper.

After a few moments, he lifted his head and looked at the students. His eyes delivered the message before the words could leave his mouth.

"I'm afraid this isn't good," he said. "If what's written here is accurate, then the creature named Blahbbity Blah Blah is supposed to awaken after 10,000 years and return to his life of mayhem. Today is 10,000 years to the day."

"Impossible."

"It's all here: 'With our remaining resources, we could not destroy the Blahbbity Blah Blah. It is believed that the capsule in which we imprisoned the Blahbbity Blah Blah will run out of operating power after 3,650,000 rotations of our planet. After that, the Blahbbity Blah Blah will begin drawing energy from any nearby organisms, recharge his system, and finally awaken.' "

It felt like all of time had frozen.

" 'To our comrades in the future, we hope that you receive our gift and, with its help, succeed in eradicating the Blahbbity Blah Blah off the face of our precious Earth.' According to my friend's translation, the plate can be dated to 10,000 years ago. Given that 3,650,000 days works out to be ten millennia, we can only assume . . ."

"That it's *today?*"

"You have to be joking."

RUMBLE. RUMBLE. RUMBLE.

Small tremors, not unlike the preamble of an earthquake, shook through the Back Hill. Then, just as suddenly as they had started, they stopped.

"What was that?"

The sudden trembling had caused Yuki to lose his balance.

"W-what's going on? What's with all the shaking?" he shouted.

The tunnel filled with the smoke from Yuki's torch. He squared himself off, bracing his hands on the opposite walls and steeling himself for what was necessary.

"*Senpai!*" Rion called to him from outside the pit.

"What is it?"

"L-look!"

Yuki poked his head back out of the hole. What Rion had wanted him to see was right in front of him, as big as Tokyo Tower. A gigantic column of dirt was rising into the air from the densely forested area beyond the Back Hill.

"What is *that?*"

As it reached its peak, the column snapped. The dirt fell to the ground with a loud thud. Dirt was flying everywhere, small specks of it hitting Yuki and Rion in the face.

And then . . .

SHAAAAAAGYAAAAAAAAAA!!

What *was* that?"

When the dirt settled, a huge, menacing creature, standing nearly twenty meters high, emerged from the dust.

"Oh, my . . . !"

Sakiko was watching the events unfold from the rooftop of the Professor's building. She swallowed hard on a big chunk of nerves.

Although she was in the university district, which shared a border with the grade school, the full territory of CLAMP School was so vast that more than a kilometer separated the two sections. From this distance, the monster appeared to be no bigger than a harmless toy, but Sakiko knew better. In her eyes, the creature looked to be as tall as the heavens, big enough to swat at the sun.

A portentous wind kicked up and started to blow across CLAMP School. It carried the shouts and screams of the students like litter over the campus.

The gust was strong, and Sakiko grabbed onto the security fence, afraid her whole life might be blown away.

Sakiko feared that the tremor everyone had felt was merely a prologue for the horrific things to come, as if this creature had merely been announcing itself. Sakiko's heart began to ache with something she could not put a name on. Frightened by the rumbling, she ran out of the research lab and did not stop until she had reached the roof.

"*Sakiko-chan!*"

Koji burst through the door and found Sakiko with her fingers tightly wrapped around the links in the fence.

"This is a dangerous place to be!" he shouted. "We have to get out of here!"

The monster's presence had shifted Koji's protective instinct into overdrive.

"*Koji-san!*" Sakiko cried out.

His own name sounded alien to him. It caused Koji to pause before he replied, "What?"

"It's not him!" Sakiko almost sounded ecstatic.

"W-what are you talking about?"

"It's not him! That's not *Zetton!*"

"Huh?"

The words spilled out of his mouth. In the back of his brain, Koji wondered if this were what it felt like to be struck dumb.

"Are you sure? That's *not* Zetton? *Really?*"

"Uh-huh! I'm positive! That's not my Zetton! It's something else!"

Sakiko's cheeks were still wet with tears, but now, rather than despair, she had a big, satisfied smile on her face. Seeing it, Koji breathed a sigh of relief.

I'm glad. So glad that Sakiko-chan's pet isn't the Blahbbity Blah Blah after all. Finally, her sadness can come to an end.

For the first time in three days, Koji's entire body relaxed.

But it wasn't meant to last.

Forget the feeling. The very word *relaxed* was violently ripped from his mind.

Whoa. That means the monster running through the grade school is in fact the Blahbbity Blah Blah. That's not good. No . . . it's awful!

Every hair on Koji's body had risen to attention. He felt like he had swallowed a battery and it was short-circuiting in his stomach.

෨ ෨

"Chairman! Let's get out of here! It's going to be a little hard to study the monster when it's tearing everything apart."

Rion looked at Yuki with eyes made of steel— showing an unusual assertiveness.

"Y-you're right," Yuki stammered. "I a-agree."

Although he had expended an immense amount of effort finding this creature, Yuki quickly calculated the pros and cons of trying to ensure the survival of the Association versus saving his own skin, and the equation had only one possible answer.

And if he didn't believe his own math, the huge, scary-looking horn on top of the monster's head presented an irrefutable argument.

"It's really too bad. . . . If we could take the time to really study this specimen, our Association would be on the fast track to becoming a Club, no problem."

"Y-yeah, well . . . another time maybe."

SHAGYAAAAAAAAAH.

A hot wind sliced through the field atop the Back Hill like a burning scythe.

"Hey . . . !"

As if it wanted to make its position clear, the monster unleashed an earth-shaking howl. It then thrashed its head from left to right. Finally it stopped, settling its sights to the west, like it had spotted something. Slowly it raised itself up on its hind legs and began moving westward. With each step, there was an enormous BOOM that shook Yuki and Rion to their core.

"Where is it going?" Yuki wondered. "It seems to be clearing a path to the west."

"That's the direction of the kindergarten campus, isn't it?" questioned Rion.

The pair stared at each other, puzzled. Just what did all this mean?

"What's it doing?" Koji asked. "Could it be heading to the kindergarten? 'Cause that's what it looks like."

Sakiko's expression suggested she knew more than she was saying.

They were still on the rooftop, watching it all with the advantage of both height and distance. This turn of events seemed totally random . . . but at the same time also painstakingly planned.

"Maybe . . ." Koji murmured. "Maybe it's looking for something . . . ?"

Sakiko was sure of it now.

"That direction," she gasped, "it's . . . !"

"What is it, Sakiko-chan?"

Koji had been staring so intently at the spectacle of the monster, he hadn't noticed the change in his friend.

"If it keeps going that way, it's going to end up at Genbu Park."

"What?"

Sakiko turned to Koji, her eyes filled with panic. "Don't you get it? The monster is looking for Zetton. Don't ask me how I know. . . . I just feel it. I'm sure that's what it's doing."

She clutched her chest. "Koji-san," she said, looking him straight in the eye. "Please, do something. That monster is going to destroy Zetton's . . . Zetton's *pond!*"

"Sakiko-chan . . . but what *can* I do?"

Koji was completely at a loss.

Yet, he was also at a loss for a way around Sakiko's pleading eyes. He knew that he had to do *something*, even if he wasn't sure what. Swallowing his fear, Koji dashed for the exit.

"Wait! Koji-kun!"

The others heard Koji bounding down the stairs. The Professor and Takayuki jumped out of the lab and blocked the ninja's path.

"Please, get out of my way. I have to . . . I have to stop him."

"There's no way you'll make it in time," the Professor said. Oddly enough, he was smiling, and the squareness of his shoulders hinted at a newfound confidence. "Besides, I have an idea. Let me show you."

Back up on the rooftop, the Professor dramatically tore away a waterproof sheet, unveiling an unusual piece of machinery. Long and shaped like a cicada, it was a vehicle of some kind, harnessed to the rooftop.

The Professor began to unhook the vehicle. He then spread out two wings that had been tucked along the length of its body. He looked like a father showing off his newborn.

"This is a man-powered airplane, propelled by pedaling. I developed it as a lark along with some of the guys over in the Aeronautic Department."

"A *man-powered* airplane?"

The members, for the umpteenth time, couldn't believe what they were seeing.

"You just push this lever forward, and pedal as hard and fast as you can. Under normal manpower, you can keep the vehicle in the air for about twenty minutes. It all depends on a favorable wind and, of course, the cooperation of gravity."

Koji's voice shot up a couple of octaves. "Y-you expect me to fly to Genbu Park in this contraption?"

"That's right. Come on, there's no time to be a nervous Nellie. Hop in the backseat."

Grabbing the helmet from inside the cockpit and fastening the jaw strap under his chin, the Professor slid into the front.

"Me, too! Please take me, too!" Sakiko rushed forward, grabbing the Professor by his white coat.

"What?" Koji said. "That's impossible. It's too dangerous for you, Sakiko-chan."

Koji watched helplessly as all of his efforts to protect the poor girl dissolved.

"There are only two seats," the Professor said. "If you want to go along for the ride, then Koji-kun is going to have to hold you tight."

"You got it!" Sakiko didn't wait for Koji to agree. She jumped right onto his lap in the backseat.

Those cheeks of Koji's, the ones all the girls found so pinchable, began to blush again. He adjusted himself in the seat, and wrapped his arms around Sakiko—as per the Professor's instructions.

Takayuki took position on the catapult platform. He checked the wind speed and directional gauges. "Professor!" he reported. "The wind speed is three meters. Conditions are extremely favorable."

"Okay, kids, have you fastened your seatbelts?"

"Yes, sir!"

"All right, then, let's *blast off!*"

CLUNK!

WHOOSH!

In a matter of seconds, the trio was in mid-flight, sailing twenty meters above the ground.

"Whaa—?"

Mifuyu's skirt flapped under the force of the headwind.

Moments before Koji and the others were thrust into the air, Mifuyu had begun running with all her might along the road leading to the pond.

With her right hand, she had drawn her sword, the Kotetsu, which had, as always, been strapped to her back.

Takayuki had ordered her to secure Genbu Park before Koji's expedition could arrive. Mifuyu was determined to push her legs as hard as they could go, in order to beat the plane to the water's edge.

Let's just hope Sakiko-chan's pet was smart enough to get the heck out of there.

Even running like a demon couldn't stop Mifuyu's strange little brain from rambling.

"Whoa, whoa, whoa!"

SLAMMMMMMM.

The Professor erupted in a hearty laugh. "Looks like I miscalculated the distance by a hair or two, but any landing you can walk away from is a good one."

The plane had come to ground—or, rather, to branch—up in the row of trees that dotted the park. The Professor giggled in his pilot's seat, high on the adrenaline of flight.

"Owwwww," Koji moaned. "Sakiko-chan, are you all right?"

"Uh-huh."

Sakiko carefully climbed out of the backseat. Koji held her around the waist, lending her support. She grabbed a tree limb and lowered herself to the ground.

"Be careful," Koji warned, struggling with the seatbelt still wrapped around his torso. "The Lifestyle-Monitoring Committee might still have Genbu Park sealed off."

"Oh, don't you worry about that."

A familiar voice came to them from across the foliage as Sakiko broke into a trot toward the pond.

"*Mizukagami-san . . . ?*"

Sakiko was thrilled to see Mifuyu smiling and waving to her from the edge of the water.

But what was that at her feet?

"Oh, dear!"

All around Mifuyu lay seven male students, dressed in uniform and positioned back-to-back. They formed a jagged circle, and ranged from unconscious to overwhelmingly dizzy.

"Ugh . . . nnnng . . ."

"I'm guessing, they're either members of the Lifestyle-Monitoring Committee or part of the security force. Don't worry, I merely tapped them with the back of my sword. I just wanted to knock them out a bit." Mifuyu smiled, pleased with herself.

As Sakiko approached the bank of the pond, she felt a twinge of tension at her spine. "Zetton!" she cried. "*Zetton!*"

She squatted down by the water.

There was no answer.

"Zetton, *please!* Come out!"

CLUNK.

Far away, over by the low bridge, the duck-shaped boats gently bumped noses.

BOOM.

A ripple.

And then . . . the trembling.

"Sakiko-chan! Get out of there!"

BOOM.

Another ripple.

"Please, Zetton. Please come out!"

More trembling.

Several ripples.

And then . . . a dreadful silence.

SHAGYAAAAAAAAAAAAAAAAAAAHHH!

"Sakiko-chan. It's too dangerous. We need to get away from here." Koji grabbed the girl's shoulder and shook her.

"No! I can't . . . !"

Sakiko refused to budge. Hot tears were forming in her eyes.

"Sing a song!" the Professor shouted. He dropped to the ground, having finally dislodged himself from the plane's treetop airstrip. "Try anything! Sing whatever song Zetton likes!"

"W-what? Why?"

"Just trust me! Sing as loud as you can!"

Koji thought the Professor had completely lost his marbles in the crash, but Sakiko got the message. She stood up and—with fierce determination burning across her face—she folded her hands. Then, she separated them, and closed them again. She was clapping.

"Fold your hands, open them up. Clap your hands out loud. Fold your hands," she sang.

Koji was overwhelmed by the absurdity of the situation. He almost stumbled to the ground.

"Louder!" the Professor yelled. "Loud enough to be heard at the bottom of the pond!"

BOOM.

"Hurry!"

Koji had no idea what was happening, but why fight it?

"Fold your hands, open them up. Clap your hands out loud. Fold your hands."

"Open your hands again. Clap them one more time. Hold your hands up high!"

Where once there had been only a timid girl's solo there was now a mighty male-female duet reverberating throughout Genbu Park.

SPLOOSH.

SHAAGYAAAAAHHHHHH!

"We're so close. I can feel it."

SPLASHHHHHHH!

"Zeeeeettoooooooooooon!!"

"Aaaaghhhhhh!"

Timed perfectly with the mysterious scream, a huge splash of water rained on the group stationed by the shore.

"W-what *is* that?"

Miharu, Chairman of the Lifestyle-Monitoring Committee, was watching from the window of her office in the student body hall on the high school part of campus. "Now there are *two* monsters? How did this happen? It has to be some kind of hoax."

Another member of the committee burst through the door, possessed by panic.

"Chairman! We've received an SOS from one of our committee members stationed at Genbu Park. What are your orders?"

"Tell them to retreat. They need to get out of there. Is that plan simple enough for you to get right?" Gripped by hysteria, Miharu didn't know what she was saying even as the words came out of her mouth.

"Zeeeeettoooooooooooon!!"

As if the high-pitched yowl had triggered a reflex, Koji and the other three all looked up to the sky at the same time.

There they saw . . . a huge head, short legs, and a squat, chubby body.

And finally, along its back, a row of bumps unlike any they had seen on a living being before—or since.

"Aaaaaaaaaghhhh!"

Mifuyu was the first to scream.

"Those bumps! They are the three humps that students keep seeing in the water!"

"*Zetton!*" Sakiko shouted. Her throat was becoming raw from all the yelling.

"Zeeeeettoooooooooooon!!" the creature from the pond howled by way of an answer.

But its voice wasn't scary. It was actually the most adorable thing any of them had ever heard, and it seemed ridiculous to call anything that sounded like that—a monster.

"Wow, is that really him?" Koji asked. "That's the pet you raised in the washbowl?"

"Yup, that's my cuddle bunny," Sakiko replied. "I'm sure of it. He's bigger then when I dropped him off, but I'd recognize that cute face anywhere."

"Th-that's *really* him?" Koji said again. He stared sheepishly at the thing that had occupied his thoughts so completely for the last forty-eight hours. "You said he was adorable, but I didn't know you meant ultra-super-adorable."

Koji felt silly all of a sudden, but he could hardly be blamed for it.

No matter how much menace an ancient prophecy might drape Zetton in, there was no way modern eyes could look at him and not see a character from a children's TV show.

"Zeeetttooooon!"

To top off his cutesy image, his voice rivaled that of top *anime* actresses for sheer sugary sweetness.

"S-so this is the bio-weapon created to destroy the big bad Blahbbity Blah Blah," teased Miharu.

"I suppose the ancient people figured that just because a weapon was highly destructive, it didn't mean it couldn't be beautiful." Even though he was soaked from head to toe, the Professor spoke with absolute seriousness. "There was more to the message. It said, 'When the Blahbbity Blah Blah arises from his deep slumber, the song of a young girl will signal its return.' The silver plate was kind of a Zetton instruction manual. It didn't say anything about how big he was going to get, though."

"He looks like something out of a Toho monster movie," Mifuyu said, "only, like, kind of cute, too."

"Shaagyaaaaahh!"

"Zeeettooooon!"

The two ancient creatures howled across the campus at each other.

Although he was a good five meters shorter than the Blahbbity Blah Blah, Zetton was ready to fight.

Stopping in its tracks, the Blahbbity Blah Blah maintained a cautious distance. It glared across the expanse at its foe.

A monster battle of epic proportions, two behemoths pummeling each other to a pulp, was about to take place on the grade school grounds of the CLAMP School campus.

CRACKKKK!

SLAMMMMMM!

"Yikes! What was that? What's going on?"

Miharu could only see the gargantuan bodies hurtling at her for an instant before everything went dark, their shadows falling across her. The next thing she knew, she found herself trapped under a collapsing ceiling.

"The high school student body hall!" she exclaimed, "What just happened?"

Zetton charged forward blindly, only to be instantly knocked back by the Blahbbity Blah Blah's kick.

It was just one kick. But it knocked the cute critter across campus as if it were a balloon caught by a blowing fan.

"Zeeettooooon . . . !"

Zetton felt dizzy. The student body hall roof was spinning beneath him, just as it was starting to cave in. The tip of his broken tail floated haphazardly through the sky.

Koji felt his heart sink.

"H-he's weak. . . . Zetton doesn't have his full strength!"

Zetton's owner knew her pet like the back of her hand. None of the changes the creature underwent escaped her view, so when a new one appeared—a red flicker peeking out from inside his mouth—Sakiko noticed it immediately.

"Koji-san! Look! Zetton's mouth!"

"Huh?"

"That's fire!" the Professor shouted. He had noticed it, too, and was thrilled by the rapidly changing field of battle. "I don't know how, but there's fire burning inside Zetton's body."

Wait a minute, Koji thought, *didn't Sakiko-chan say fire was Zetton's favorite food? That's it!*

"Professor! Is it possible that Zetton can *breathe* fire?"

"Fire?"

Everyone turned to face Koji, to hear what he had to say.

"Think about it. Zetton was raised on fire. Sakiko said he *inhaled* it. Well, maybe he can *exhale* flames, as well. Could it be he was storing up fire in preparation for facing the Blahbbity Blah Blah?"

The Professor scratched his chin. "I suppose it's not completely out of the realm of possibility." Then he groaned. "But so what if you're right? Seeing how Zetton's been attacking so far, it appears he only understands how to fight with his body. I don't think he knows that he can blow the fire, and I don't know how we're going to be able to tell him."

"Well . . ." Koji looked back toward the student body hall.

"Hurm?" After it had knocked Zetton down with one kick, the Blahbbity Blah Blah stopped and looked about curiously. Perhaps it expected there was another monster waiting somewhere, that certainly its 10,000-year-old foe wasn't *this* wimpy.

But, no, it was clear Zetton was the only other monster around. The Blahbbity Blah Blah resumed its advance.

This time, it was going to finish off Zetton for good.

Hold on, Zetton! I'll get your fires roaring!

Climbing to the rooftop of the student body hall, Koji quickly tossed his daggers into the cracks that had developed in the roof and walls. Once the ninja star had opened the cracks wide enough, he followed with firebombs.

"We just have to push on Zetton's stomach," Koji had said.

"But how?" Mifuyu asked.

"We have to drop something heavy on him. Like the roof of the student body hall."

Now that he had a plan, nothing was going to stop Koji from putting it into action.

I can't abandon Zetton. I must do this, for Sakiko-chan's sake.

"Koji-kun!" Mifuyu called up to him from the ground below. "Here comes the monster!"

Koji turned to look. The Blahbbity Blah Blah was slowly changing direction, its gargantuan body lumbering Koji's way.

"Okay! Get out of the way, Mizukagami-senpai! Get someplace safe!"

"Good luck!"

Koji waited until Mifuyu was able to take cover, and then he jumped down onto the rooftop.

Zetton was still slumped against the building, dizzy and groaning.

This better work.

Gripping the trigger string, Koji closed his eyes.

Suddenly, at that moment, Zetton woke up.

He had sensed the Blahbbity Blah Blah's approach. His instinct was kicking in. He had to get up.

"Zetton! No! Stay where you are!!"

The Professor and Sakiko had retreated to the artificial garden on the edge of the high school. Seeing her beloved pet about to ruin Koji's plan, she shrieked in alarm.

She could have screamed as loud as she wanted. Zetton was never going to hear her. He had gone into full battle mode.

"Now!"

Koji pulled the string with all his might.

There was a pause. It hung in the air like a star about to fall.

The firebombs exploded, detonating in rapid succession. The damaged walls and columns crumbled and split, while the debris blew in every direction.

The bursts from the bombs spread, and the roof, with its weakened foundation, began to cave under its own weight.

"Aggggh! Nooooo!"

"Zeeettooooon . . . !"

"Shaagyaaaaahh!"

The two foes once again faced each other, their eyes locked. Who would blink first?

Right at that moment, the broken roof of the student body hall plummeted to the ground. The rumble of the collapse was deep and low. And, by the way the smoke and dust swirled, it looked like everything was happening in slow motion.

The roof was heading directly for Zetton's tail.

CRASH!

"Zeeeeeeeeeettooooooooon!"

WHOOMPH!

A huge fireball began to form deep within Zetton's throat. The flame swirled around itself, gathering, expanding, until it had reached nearly three meters in diameter.

"Shagyahhh?"

The fireball slammed into the Blahbbity Blah Blah, shattering into a pinwheel of sparks. The monster's body burst into flame.

It took only a second for the fire to engulf the behemoth's entire body, and just a moment more for it to disintegrate. A molten plasma scattered into the air, soon carried away by the wind.

"Yeah!"

"Zeeeeettoooooooon!"

Koji didn't speak Zetton's language, but he was pretty sure the creature was boasting.

The victory cheer didn't last.

As the final boiling drops of Blahbbity Blah Blah rained onto the CLAMP School campus, Zetton started to change.

"Zeee . . . zee. . . Zeeeeettoooon?!"

"Zetton! What's happening?!" Sakiko cried out from the garden.

"This isn't good," the Professor said. "Now that we've stoked the fire, it's beginning to leak from his entire body."

VWOOSH!

Just as they got out of one hot situation, the students found themselves in another—fire was erupting from all over Zetton.

As the flames ran wild, the group ran toward one another for comfort.

"Zeeeeeettooooooooon!"

FWOOOOOOM!

Zetton blasted from the ground, shooting high into the sky like a rocket, howling the whole way.

It was like he'd been a balloon, and someone had deflated it.

"Committee Chairman Miharu! Are you all right? Is anything broken?" asked the Professor.

Rescue workers were pushing aside the rubble in what was left of the student body hall, searching for survivors. Luckily for the Chairman, her desk served as a shelter from the crushing debris. Miharu had escaped without a single scratch.

". . . what happened . . . w-what was that . . . ?"

Her body had suffered no injury. But the fright of the situation, the shock of the explanations of science failing her—these caused emotional wounds that weren't going to heal anytime soon.

After things settled down, repair on the student body hall and Genbu Park began in earnest. The efficient CLAMP School maintenance team went into action, and everything was tidied up without delay. Within two days, it was impossible to tell anything out of the ordinary had happened at all.

Once the facts were reviewed, the Student Body Executive Committee ruled that the monster in the pond caused the fire at Genbu Park. Koji was declared innocent. The Supernatural Phenomena Research Association was allowed to continue—albeit unofficially.

Of course, no one would know of the involvement of a certain young girl, and how just maybe she had added fuel to the fire in question.

"It's beautiful, isn't it, Sakiko-chan?"

"Uh-huh."

Three days had passed since Zetton had his showdown with Blahbbity Blah Blah.

Koji had invited Sakiko to the rooftop of the university building, where they held a regular "Stargazing for Two" night.

Zetton had so much excess energy that he couldn't contain it. It ruptured his shell and catapulted him into the stratosphere. Sakiko had since become glum, and at the Professor and Takayuki's urging, Koji had asked her out in hopes of cheering her up.

"I wonder what Zetton is doing now?" she pondered.

"Hmmm . . . well, Zetton *is* an artificial creature, after all," Koji said. "When he's low on energy he might go back into hibernation, maintaining an orbit until he's ready to come back down."

Sakiko was silent. Her eyes were sad, even as they reflected the nighttime sky. Then, finally, she smiled. "I want to be an astronaut when I grow up," she said, turning to Koji. "That way, when I go into outer space, I'll be able to visit him."

"That's a good idea. I bet Zetton would like that."

The two smiled at each other, then turned back to the star field spread out before them. The breeze glided over their blushing cheeks, cooling them down.

"Phew," Yuki breathed a sigh of relief. "Now that the arson charge has been dismissed, the Association will be able to pick up where it left off. I guess all really is well that ends well."

The Association meetings were back on—same time, same place.

"I suppose," Takayuki said as he wiped the sweat from his glasses. "I swear . . . when that second monster showed up, I was scared to death. I had no idea what was going to happen."

Mifuyu folded her arms. "But," she wondered, "why did the Blahbbity Blah Blah come out of the Back Hill like that? One second he wasn't there, and the next—*Rahhhhhh!*"

"Oh, that was because the Chairman set a fire—"

"Shh! *Shhhh!*" Yuki jumped to his feet, waving for Rion to shut up. "Oh, uh, that monster came to battle Zetton. It was destiny, you know? Just like in those old monster movies. The instinct to fight completely took over.

"Powerful beings can naturally sense when their enemies are near, and so he had no choice but to rise up and do battle. Yeah, that's it.

"Let's leave it at that, shall we?"

It was an early summer evening on the Back Hill. The tiny voices of the insects could be heard in the grass.

There was no need to rush things. The various members of the Association had plenty of time to come up with a good way of telling their newest tale. . . .

Epilogue

The large body slammed to the ground.

"T-Takayuki–dono, my sword! Please, return my sword to me!"

Takayuki did as requested, and handed the sword back to the kindergartener. The child was looking past him, preparing to stand guard against the thunder spirit.

"*Seeeeeiiiii!*"

It was a death scream. Aptly named, too, because it was bloodcurdling.

The spirit split in half, and rather pathetically, it dissipated into the air.

"Y-you did it. . . ." Takayuki collapsed to the ground.

Yuki laughed wearily. "We finally killed it," he said, panting heavily.

"Man . . ." Koji sighed.

He and Mifuyu were carrying Rion, who was unconscious. Once they were where they needed to be, they both dropped down, landing on their butts, exhausted.

"Ay yi yi . . . I sure am sick of these spirits." Koji confessed.

The high school division of CLAMP School was in a rebuilding mode.

At their usual gathering place at the entrance to the roof, Yuki was conducting a meeting.

"Anyway, because of what happened, the Subway Wish Fulfillment Ritual has been forbidden. Security at the ticket gates has been tightened. So it looks like it's going to be impossible to carry on with the investigation."

"I doubt it would be necessary to, anyway," Takayuki countered. "The fact that the administration acknowledged the vows enough to ban them means we proved the ritual was real."

"It's not enough for them to acknowledge the phenomenon," Yuki said, "They have to acknowledge that the Supernatural Phenomena Research Association were the ones who uncovered it. If they don't, we get nothing out of it. What about our credibility?"

"Yeah, but if we got the credit for uncovering the ritual," Mifuyu said, indulging in a rare protest, "then we'd also get the blame for waking up the monster. Would it be worth it?"

"She's right," Koji agreed. "Right now, our names have stayed out of the affair. So why stir up trouble?"

Rion agreed with the others, but she didn't say anything.

"All right, already!" Yuki said. His voice expressed an equal mixture of hurt and anger. "Fine! I give up. We'll just move on to the next case, okay? Happy? Consider the matter closed, as if it never happened!"

A Word from the Author

Hmmm . . . ? Where am I?

I was busy doing some research in a private room at the university building, and the next thing I know . . . how did I end up in this huge place?

Oh, wait! This is that space in the book for an afterword and stuff. I didn't realize it at first.

Okay, I'm taking off the Professor hat and putting on the one for Commentator.

So, anyway, as you can see, the first installment of *CLAMP School Paranormal Investigators* has now concluded.

First off, all the members of Supernatural Phenomena Research Association originally appeared in the now-defunct magazine *Shosetsu Asuka*. The whole thing was initially inspired by a creative game that the members of CLAMP used to play among themselves. Each of these characters was based on a member of the studio, so you can consider this to be an extravagant exercise in self-mythology.

Due to the favorable response the stories received, the characters were brought back for several more episodes. If you were reading along and suddenly thought that maybe you'd missed something, or that the narrative seemed to be the continuation of an earlier story, now you know why.

If you are interested in those earlier episodes, check out Asuka Comic DX *The Official CLAMP School Guidebook*, as well as *This Is the CLAMP School Supernatural Phenomena Research Association #1* from Asuka Novels.

Now then, allow me to explain a bit about the stories recorded in this book.

Some of you readers may be confused as to why there is an extra story broken up into incomplete chapters called "Prologue," "Intermission," and "Epilogue." Let me explain.

This story is an abstract of a previously published story titled *The Phantom Fourth Story*. If I listed all the previously published *CLAMP School Supernatural Phenomena Research Association* stories in chronological order, it would go something like this:

Episode 0—Published titles: *The Cursed Ice Cream; We Thus Investigate the Supernatural*
Episode 1—*The Mysterious O-Parts (Out-of-Place Artifacts)*
Episode 2—*The Messenger from the Ruins*
Episode 3—*The Dreaming Mummy*

Episode 4 (new)—*The Still Ghost* (first published as *This Is the CLAMP School Supernatural Phenomena Research Association*)
Episode 5 (new)—*The Invader from Space*
Episode 6 (new)—The story broken up from the "Prologue" through the "Epilogue"
Episode 7 (new)—*A Gift from the Past*

Have you noticed that Episode four and beyond are indicated as "new"? Well, between Episode three and Episode four there are previously unreleased stories, which were included in the archival books. And that includes the phantom Episode four, *The Subway Monster.*

Although I'm sure you can figure out the story from reading this book (ha ha), I thought it would be good to reintroduce Episode four. I received lots of mail about it, and revisited it in order to make sense of the plotlines that continue in Episode eight and beyond. In addition, I have a lot of personal attachment to that Episode four, and I didn't want it to simply fade away. Therefore, I chose to leave the plotline in this novel, and thus resurrected it in the form you see here. (Although, I could have resolved the loose ends by simply eliminating and revising the other stories.)

I did my best to write these stories down in a way that would be easily understood, but stumbled some due to limitations in page count and formats.

Please forgive me for sections that I have not been able to fill in completely (ha ha, again).

In regard to the overall content, as you saw in this book, and will no doubt see again in future ones, I will develop stories that will feature each individual member of the Association. Since I've already written stories featuring the entire group, I thought it might be a good idea to concentrate on each one individually.

In the next book, since they didn't get much of the spotlight this time around, I will have stories that star Mifuyu, Rion, and Takayuki, focusing on their individual areas of expertise. Just as I hope you enjoyed this novel's stories of Yuki and Koji, I also hope you dig your other favorite characters in their future exploits. Stay tuned!

So, anyway, I think this monologue has run its course.

I need to be getting back to my research, regardless.

If you need anything, feel free to visit me in the university division. Goodbye.

1999, August.

CLAMP School TRPG Club: Supervising Advisor
"The Professor," Tomoyuki Matsumoto.

STOP!

This is the end of the story.
For bonus manga short,
go straight to page 182.

The following pages are printed "manga-style," in the authentic Japanese right-to-left format. Since none of the artwork has been flipped or altered, readers get to experience the story just as the creator intended. You've been asking for it, so TOKYOPOP® delivered: authentic, hot-off-the-press, and far more fun!

DIRECTIONS

If this is your first time reading manga-style, here's a quick guide to help you understand how it works.

It's easy... just start in the top right panel and follow the numbers. Have fun, and look for more 100% authentic manga from TOKYOPOP®!

THANKFULLY, A HANDSOME YOUNG BOY WAS THERE TO PICK IT UP FOR ME.

Funny, I can't recall his face.

I WAS TAKING A WALK WITH MY PARASOL...

...WHEN THE WIND BLEW MY RIBBON AWAY.

AREN'T MY MEMORIES ABSOLUTELY ROMANTIC?! ♡

Right?

THAT'S LIKE SOMETHING OUT OF A YOUNG GIRLS' MANGA.

GUESS WHAT? WE WERE ALL SAYING WE SHOULD GO TO MY CABIN FOR SUMMER VACATION!

Hey! There they are!

THE END

175

SO, ANYWAY, LET ME FINISH MY STORY!

ONLY GOOD THINGS, OF COURSE!

MAYBE YOU *DO* HAVE SOME KIND OF VIRUS.

HA-CHOO!

THE ONE ABOUT GOING TO YOUR FAMILY'S CABIN IN THE SUMMER?

I'M TELLING YOU, *SOMEBODY'S* TALKING ABOUT ME!

I'm fine!

Hmm...

Oh!

OF COURSE NOT! I'LL BE YOUR HOSTESS!

WHY DON'T ALL OF US IN THE SUPER-NATURAL PHENOMENA RESEARCH ASSOCIATION GO TOGETHER?

UH-HUH! I GO THERE EVERY SUMMER TO GET AWAY FROM THE HEAT.

THAT'S RIGHT! I JUST REMEMBERED! I HAVE A GREAT STORY ABOUT SOMETHING NICE THAT HAPPENED THERE WHEN I WAS IN THE FOURTH GRADE.

WOULDN'T WE BE IN THE WAY?

THANK YOU.

The end.

NO. I NEVER SAW HER AGAIN.

It's been so long, I've forgotten her face.

SO, DIDJA ASK HER OUT?

WHAT A BEAUTIFUL STORY!!

ESPECIALLY WITH WHO WE HAVE AS CHAIRMAN.

NOT THAT IT MATTERS, BUT...THERE'S NO ROOM FOR LOVE IN OUR LITTLE GROUP.

...in the fourth Karuizawa... ...at little ji... ...the parasol... with a parasol...

EVEN SO, YOU'RE QUITE THE ROMANTIC, SENPAI.

LET'S
SEE...

IT
HAPPENED
ON SUMMER
VACATION
WHEN I WAS
IN THE
FOURTH
GRADE.

MY
FAMILY
WENT TO
KARUIZAWA
TO ESCAPE
THE HEAT...

Memories...

Hmmm...

NAH. SOMEONE IS TALKING ABOUT HOW PRETTY I AM, THAT'S ALL.

DO YOU HAVE A COLD?

ARE YOU ALL RIGHT?

HA-CHOO!

WELL, I DOUBT ANY GIRL WOULD BE UNHAPPY IF YOU SENT HER *ANY* OF THOSE THINGS.

FLOWERS...

Candy, stuffed animals, flowers

CANDY, STUFFED ANIMALS...

I'VE GOT TO HAND IT TO YOU, USAGIYA-SENPAI: YOU'RE NOT JUST BOOK SMART, BUT YOU'VE GOT AN UNDERSTANDING OF THE WAYS OF THE WORLD.

THIS IS GREAT!

Let me write that down.

IF IT'S TOO TACKY OR NOT HER STYLE, SHE'LL TOSS YOU ASIDE IN NO TIME FLAT.

JEWELRY IS OUT OF THE QUESTION.

We're the only two guys in the Association, after all! Well, unless we count...

I JUST WANT TO KNOW AS A REFERENCE POINT.

WHY ARE YOU CHANGING THE SUBJECT?

WHO WAS *YOUR* FIRST LOVE, USAGIYA SENPAI?

So...

CLAMP SCHOOL
PARANORMAL INVESTIGATORS

This is CLAMP School Supernatural Phenomena Research Association
* Illustrations from the comic CLAMP (pp. 175-182)

OH! USAGIYA-SENPAI!!

He's in charge of snacks.

CLAMP School Supernatural Phenomena Research Association Room (actually, the stairwell)

WHAT IS IT, TAKAMURA?

I HAVE A DILEMMA.

No, even though I do suck at school.

DID SOMETHING HAPPEN? DID YOU CRASH AND BURN ON YOUR TESTS?

WHY SO GLUM, CHUM?

YOU MEAN SAKIKO-CHAN FROM THE ZETTON INCIDENT?

IT'S SAKIKO-CHAN'S BIRTHDAY TOMORROW, AND I DON'T KNOW WHAT TO GET HER.

Welcome back to CLAMP School, where mystery and adventure abound. *Volume 2* reunites the infamous Paranormal Investigators, still determined to become an official Club. To this end, Chairman Yuki assigns Rion to write a report, chronicling all the past activities of the Association.

The Paranormal Investigators leave no stone unturned as they strive to solve each and every unexplained phenomenon rocking the CLAMP campus. Following the Haunted Tree Mystery, the Association sets off to uncover the "scoop" on the killer ice cream. And, when Mifuyu and Rion team up for the school treasure hunt, little do they expect the real prize awaiting them at the finish. As if that's not enough for the illustrious quintet, the Paranormal Investigators get caught in a never-ending loop, with the same day repeating itself over and over. With this glitch in the time/space continuum, there's no telling who might get trapped . . . indefinitely.

ALSO AVAILABLE FROM  TOKYOPOP®

MANGA

ALSO AVAILABLE FROM TOKYOPOP

WHODUNNIT?

THE **KINDAICHI** CASE FILES ™

BY: YOZABURO KANARI & FUMIYA SATO

TOKYOPOP ®

HAJIME KINDAICHI IS ON THE CASE!

AVAILABLE NOW AT YOUR FAVORITE
BOOK AND COMIC STORES

T TEEN AGE 13+

www.TOKYOPOP.com

When darkness is in your genes,
only love can steal it away.

TOKYOPOP

D·N·ANGEL·

The One I Love

watashi no suki na hito

FROM CLAMP CREATORS OF CHOBITS & TOKYO BABYLON

breathtaking stories of love and romance

SUKI™

A like story...

by CLAMP

TOKYOPOP®

T TEEN AGE 13+

www.TOKYOPOP.com

FROM CLAMP, CREATORS OF CHOBITS.

TOKYO BABYLON ™

Welcome to Tokyo.
The city never sleeps.
May its spirits rest in peace.